BASIC STUDY MANUAL

Basic Study Manual

Based on the Works of

L. RON HUBBARD

PUBLICATIONS, INC.

Published by
Bridge Publications, Inc.
4751 Fountain Avenue
Los Angeles, California 90029

ISBN 0-88404-631-1

© 1992
L. Ron Hubbard Library
All Rights Reserved

Printed in the United States of America

Important Note

In reading this book, be very certain you never go past a word you do not fully understand.

The only reason a person gives up a study or becomes confused or unable to learn is because he or she has gone past a word that was not understood.

The confusion or inability to grasp or learn comes AFTER a word that the person did not have defined and understood.

Have you ever had the experience of coming to the end of a page and realizing you didn't know what you had read? Well, somewhere earlier on that page you went past a word that you had no definition for or an incorrect definition for.

Here's an example. "It was found that when the crepuscule arrived the children were quieter and when it was not present, they were much livelier." You see what happens. You think you don't understand the whole idea, but the inability to understand came entirely from the one word you could not define, *crepuscule,* which means twilight or darkness.

It may not only be the new and unusual words that you will have to look up. Some commonly used words can often be misdefined and so cause confusion.

This datum about not going past an undefined word is the most important fact in the whole subject of study. Every subject you have taken up and abandoned had its words which you failed to get defined.

Therefore, in studying this book be very, very certain you never go past a word you do not fully understand. If the material becomes confusing or you can't seem to grasp it, there will be a word just earlier that you have not understood. Don't go any further, but go back to BEFORE you got into trouble, find the misunderstood word and get it defined.

Definitions

As an aid to the reader, words most likely to be misunderstood have been defined in footnotes the first time they occur in the text. Words sometimes have several meanings. The footnote definitions in this book only give the meaning that the word has as it is used in the text. Other definitions for the word can be found in a dictionary.

A glossary including all the footnote definitions is at the back of this book. This glossary is not meant as a substitute for a dictionary.

Editors' Foreword

Just about everyone agrees that in order to better yourself and get ahead in life, you have to be able to study. Getting through school, getting a promotion on the job, making more money and other personal and professional achievements are often determined solely by the ability to study and apply what you have learned. But how does one acquire this ability?

The answer is in this practical guide to better study skills. This book contains the fundamentals of the first actual *technology* of study, developed by American writer and educator L. Ron Hubbard.

L. Ron Hubbard's study technology is being used with great enthusiasm and success by educators and students throughout the world—because it *works*. You can find this out for yourself by reading the chapters of this book in sequence and doing the drills provided. *The Basic Study Manual* can be studied at home, using paper or a notebook to write down the drill assignments, or as a classroom training course available from Applied Scholastics International.[1]

This book and its drills have been designed in such a way that if you honestly do each step, you will not only have absorbed some data that can help you, but you will be practiced in actually applying that data to get *results*.

The quality of your life depends on your ability to learn. And really learning *any* subject is made possible with this vital new technology.

The Editors

---

1. **Applied Scholastics International:** the organization which promotes and utilizes L. Ron Hubbard's study technology with the aim of restoring educational quality and effectiveness around the world. It licenses and coordinates over 150 educational centers and schools on five continents. For more information, contact Applied Scholastics International at the address in the back of this book.

Contents

CHAPTER ONE:

WHY STUDY?

Why Study?

In his dictionary[1] of 1828, Noah Webster[2] said that "to study" means "to apply the mind to; to read and examine for the purpose of learning and understanding."

Why does one study?

Until you clarify that, you cannot make an intelligent activity of it.

Some students go through a course and wind up[3] at the other end of it unable to do anything with it. In actual fact, this is because they studied the course just so they could pass the examination; they did not study the course in order to apply the data in it.

This is why such people fail in practice after they graduate.

---

1. **dictionary:** a word book. A dictionary contains the meanings of words and other information about them. A dictionary can be used to find out what a word means, how to say a word, how to spell a word, how to use a word and many other things about words.

2. **Noah Webster:** (1758–1843) American educator and author, best known for his *American Dictionary of the English Language* (1828) and a spelling book called the *Blue-Backed Speller*. A number of widely used dictionaries, of varying scope and quality, still bear Webster's name. *See also* **dictionary.**

3. **wind up:** *(informal)* arrive in a place or situation as a result of a given course of action.

Instead of thinking, "Is this going to be on the exam?" one would do much better to ask himself, "How can I apply this material?" or "How can I really use this?"

With that in mind, a person would get much more out of what he studied, and would be able to put what he studied to actual use.

Drill

1. Write down an example of a time you studied something with no intention of using the data you were studying.

2. Write down how you did on that subject. How much of it do you remember?

3. Now write down an example of something you studied for the purpose of using the data.

4. Compare your knowledge of these two subjects and write down your conclusions.

The First Obstacle to Learning

The first obstacle[4] to learning is the idea that one "knows it all already."

A student who thinks he knows all there is to know about a subject will not be able to learn anything in it.

Such a student doesn't even know what he doesn't know.

If you asked him if he was willing to learn about it, he would try to avoid your question. He isn't willing to learn about it because he has the false idea that he knows all about it already.

As an example, I once took a correspondence course[5] in photography, thinking that I might learn a few more tricks in the subject. I had been a rather successful photographer, having sold many of my photographs to magazines, and some of my work had even been published in geography[6] books. However, once I started the course, I only got as far as the third lesson when I found myself bogging[7] on it and putting it aside.

Later, I took another look at this correspondence course I was taking and realized that this same course contained the real basics and fundamentals of the subject of photography that I didn't even know existed in it. I saw that I didn't know even the first fundamental of why photographs were taken in the first place!

It dawned on me that I had been very arrogant[8] and that I really didn't know all there was to know on the subject of photography, and that there was something there to learn.

Once I could see this, I buckled down[9] and started to study the course for real. I then finished the next eight lessons in two weeks of part-time study and gained a workable[10] understanding of the subject for the first time. All the knowledge and understanding I had learned from that course would have been denied me if I had not overcome the first obstacle to learning.

---

4. **obstacle:** something that stands in the way or stops progress.

5. **correspondence course:** a course of instruction by mail, given by a school *(correspondence school)* which sends lessons and examinations to a student periodically, and corrects and grades the returned answers.

6. **geography:** of or having to do with the scientific study of the Earth's surface and its physical features, climate, products and population.

7. **bogging:** being stuck and unable to make progress.

8. **arrogant:** proud and overbearing (forcing others to one's own will) through an exaggerated feeling of one's superiority.

9. **buckled down:** set to work with real effort.

10. **workable:** able to be worked or used or acted upon successfully.

On the subject of learning itself, the first datum to learn and the first obstacle to overcome is: *"Why are you studying it if you know all about it to begin with?"*

If a student can decide that he does not already know everything about a subject and can say to himself, "Here is something to study, let's study it," he can overcome this obstacle and be able to learn it.

This is a very, very important datum for any student to learn. If he knows this and applies it, the gateway to knowledge is wide open to him.

Drill

1. Write down a description of someone you have seen or known who felt that he already knew all about some subject. How would this attitude affect the person's ability to learn something new about that subject?

2. Write down an example of a subject that you don't already know everything about.

3. Write down an example of a subject that you feel you could learn something more about.

CHAPTER TWO:

THE BARRIERS TO STUDY

Barriers to Study

It has been discovered that there are three definite barriers[1] which can block a person's ability to study and thus his ability to be educated. These barriers actually produce physical and mental reactions.

If one knows and understands what these barriers are and how to handle them, his ability to study and learn will be greatly increased.

---

1. **barriers:** things that hold apart, separate or hinder.

The First Barrier: Absence of Mass

The *mass* of a subject refers to the parts of that subject which are composed of matter and energy and which exist in the material universe. For example, if one were studying how to operate tractors, the *mass* would be an actual tractor, as opposed to the theory[2] of tractors or data on the development of tractors, etc.

Trying to educate someone without the mass that he is going to be involved with can make it very difficult for him. Imagine trying to learn how to run a tractor with no tractor to look at!

---

2. **theory:** that branch of an art or science dealing with knowledge of its principles and methods rather than with its practice. *See also* **science** in the glossary.

Such an absence of mass can actually make a student feel **squashed.**

It can make him feel **bent**,

sort of spinny,[3]

---

3. spinny: dizzy, as if one were spinning.

sort of dead,

bored,

and **exasperated**.[4]

---

4. exasperated: angry; very irritated or annoyed.

If he is studying the doingness[5] of something in which the mass is absent, this will be the result.

If one is studying about tractors, the printed page and the spoken word are no substitute for having an actual tractor there.

Photographs or motion pictures are helpful because they represent a promise or hope of the mass of a tractor.

---

5. **doingness:** the action of creating an effect. By *doing* is meant action, function, accomplishment, the attainment of goals, the fulfilling of purpose or any change of position in space.

It is important to understand that educating a person in a mass that he does not have and which is not available can produce some nonoptimum[6] physical reactions.

---

6. nonoptimum: not the most favorable or desirable; not the best.

If you were trying to teach a fellow all about tractors but you did not show him any tractors or let him experience the mass of a tractor, he would wind up with a face that felt squashed, with headaches and with his stomach feeling funny. He would feel dizzy from time to time and often his eyes would hurt.

This datum has great application. For example, if a child were studying and felt sick and it was traced[7] back to a lack of mass, the positive remedy would be to supply the mass—the object itself or a reasonable substitute—and the child's sickness could rapidly clear up.

This barrier to study—the studying of something without its mass ever being around—produces very distinctly recognizable reactions.

---

7. **traced:** followed or discovered by observing marks, tracks, pieces of evidence, etc.

Drill

Write down how you would handle these situations:

1. You have just bought a new motorcycle. It is outside and you are ready to start reading the owner's manual. Where should you study the manual? Why?

2. Your friend is learning about different types of engines but has no idea what they look like. The engines are not there to show him. How could you help him?

The Second Barrier: Too Steep a Gradient

A *gradient* is a gradual approach to something taken step by step, level by level, each step or level being, of itself, easily attainable—so that finally, quite complicated and difficult activities can be achieved with relative ease. The term *gradient* also applies to each of the steps taken in such an approach.

When one hits too steep a gradient in studying a subject, **a sort of confusion** or **reelingness**[8] results. This is the second barrier to study.

Say you were to find a person who was studying about engines and he was confused and sort of reeling.

---

8. reelingness: state, quality or instance of having a whirling feeling in one's head; being or becoming confused.

You would know that there had been too much of a jump[9] from studying one type of engine to studying a more complicated type of engine. The person did not really understand something about the first type of engine but jumped to studying the next type of engine and this was too steep a gradient for him.

The person assigns[10] all of his difficulties to the *new* type of engine.

---

9. **jump:** an abrupt change of level either upward or downward.

10. **assigns:** thinks of as caused by or coming from (a motive, reason, etc.).

But the difficulty really lies at the tail end of his study of the first engine, the engine he felt he understood.

The remedy for too steep a gradient is to cut back the gradient. Find out when the person was not confused about what he was studying and then find out what new action he undertook[11] to do. Find out what he felt he understood well just *before* he got all confused.

---

11. undertook: took upon oneself, as a task, performance, etc.; attempted.

You will find that there is something in this area—the area where he felt he understood it—which he did not really understand.

When this is cleared up, the student will be able
to progress again.

This barrier of too steep a gradient is more evident and most applicable in activities in which there is doingness involved, but it also applies in subjects that are mainly concerned with thought.

When a person is found to be terribly confused on the second action he was supposed to do, it is safe to assume that he never really understood the *first* action.

Drill

Write down how you would handle these situations:

1. You are learning how to swim. You just learned how to float in the water and now you are being taught to swim across the pool, but you are having trouble with this. What should you do?

2. Write down an example of a time that you hit too steep a gradient in studying something, or you observed someone else hitting too steep a gradient. Describe what occurred. How could you have handled this using the data in this chapter?

The Third—and Most Important—Barrier: The Misunderstood Word

The third and most important barrier to study is the misunderstood word. A misunderstood word is a word which is *not* understood or *wrongly* understood.

An entirely different set of physical reactions can occur when one reads past words he does not understand. Reading on past a word that was not understood gives one a distinctly **blank feeling** or a **washed-out feeling**.

A "not-there" feeling . . .

and a **sort of nervous hysteria**[12] can follow that.

---

12. **hysteria:** any outbreak of wild, uncontrolled excitement or feeling,
    such as fits of laughing and crying.

The confusion or inability to grasp[13] or learn comes AFTER a word that the person did not have defined and understood.

---

13. **grasp:** get hold of mentally; understand.

A misunderstood definition[14] or a not-comprehended[15] definition or an undefined word can even cause a person to give up studying a subject and leave a course or class. Leaving in this way is called a "blow."

HOW'S THAT ART COURSE?

I DROPPED IT. THE TEACHER DIDN'T KNOW ANYTHING. IT'S NOT IMPORTANT ANYWAY.

---

14. definition: a statement of the meaning of a word.

15. not-comprehended: not grasped mentally; not understood.

A person does not necessarily blow because of the other barriers to study—lack of mass or too steep a gradient. These simply produce physical phenomena.[16] But the misunderstood word can cause a student to blow.

---

16. **phenomena:** facts or occurrences or changes perceived by any of the senses or by the mind.

The misunderstood word is much more important than the other two. The misunderstood word establishes aptitude[17] and lack of aptitude and this is what psychologists have been trying to test for years without recognizing what it was.

It is the misunderstood word.

This is all that many study difficulties go back to and it produces such a vast[18] panorama[19] of mental effects that it itself is the prime[20] factor[21] involved with stupidity and many other unwanted conditions.

There is some word in the field of art that the person who is unable in that field did not define or understand, and that is followed by an inability to act in the field of art.

---

17. **aptitude:** quickness to learn or understand.

18. **vast:** very great in size, extent, amount, degree, etc.

19. **panorama:** range; amount or extent of variation.

20. **prime:** chief; most important.

21. **factor:** any of the circumstances, conditions, etc., that bring about a result.

If a person didn't have misunderstoods, his *talent* might or might not be present, but his *doingness* would be present.

We can't say that Joe would paint as *well* as Bill, but we can say that the *inability* of Joe to paint compared with the *ability* of Joe to do the motions of painting is dependent exclusively[22] and only upon definitions—exclusively and only upon definitions.

This is very important because it tells one what happens to doingness and it also tells one that the restoration[23] of doingness depends only upon the restoration of understanding of the misunderstood word.

This is very simple technology. It is a sweepingly[24] fantastic discovery in the field of education and has great application.

This discovery of the importance of the misunderstood word actually opens the gate to education. And although this one has been given last, it is the most important of the barriers to study.

---

22. **exclusively:** so as to exclude all except some particular object, subject, etc.; solely.

23. **restoration:** a bringing back to a former condition.

24. **sweepingly:** including a great deal; very broadly.

Drill

Write down how you would handle these situations:

1. You have been taking a course on how to manage your money. You have decided you do not want to continue with the course or go back to class. What should you do to handle this?

2. Your friend is learning how to sew. Her instructor is having a difficult time with her because she can't figure out how to do collars. No matter how much it is explained or demonstrated to her, she still can't get it. She is about to give up on the whole subject. How would you handle this?

CHAPTER THREE:

UNDERSTANDING WORDS

Handling Misunderstood Words

A misunderstood word will remain misunderstood until one "clears" the meaning of the word. Once the word is fully understood, it is said to be "cleared." The procedures used to locate and clear up words the student has misunderstood in his studies is called Word Clearing. There are several different methods of Word Clearing which will be covered later in this book. The first thing to learn is the exact procedure to be used in clearing any word or symbol[1] one comes across in reading or studying that he does not understand.

How to Clear a Word

1. Have a dictionary to hand[2] while reading so that you can clear any misunderstood word or symbol you come across. A simple but good dictionary can be found that does not itself contain large words within the definitions of the words which have to be cleared.

2. When you come across a word or symbol that you do not understand, the first thing to do is get a dictionary and look rapidly over the definitions to find the one which applies to the context[3] in which the word was being used. Read that definition and make up sentences using the word that way until you have a clear concept[4] of that meaning of the word. This could require ten or more sentences.

3. Then clear each of the other definitions of that word, using each one in sentences until you clearly understand each definition.

When a word has several different definitions, you cannot limit your understanding of the word to one definition only and call the word "understood." You must be able to understand the word when, at a later date, it is used in a different way.

Don't, however, clear the technical or specialized definitions (math,[5] biology,[6] etc.) or obsolete (no

---

1. **symbol:** something that could represent or stand for a thought or a thing.
2. **to hand:** within reach; near; close.

3. **context:** the words just before and after a certain word, sentence, etc., that help make clear what it means.
4. **concept:** a thought devoid of (completely without) symbols, pictures, words or sounds. It is the direct idea of something rather than its sound or symbol. *See also* **symbol.**
5. **math:** *(informal)* short for *mathematics:* the science of number, quantity and space. *See also* **science** in the glossary.
6. **biology:** the science of living things; study of plant and animal life. *See also* **science** in the glossary.

longer used) or archaic (ancient and no longer in general use) definitions unless the word is being used that way in the context where it was misunderstood.

4. The next thing to do is to clear the derivation, which is the explanation of where the word came from originally. This will help you gain a basic understanding of the word.

5. Most dictionaries give the idioms of a word. An idiom is a phrase or expression whose meaning cannot be understood from the ordinary meanings of the words. For example, *all in* is an English idiom meaning "very tired." (In a sentence this might be used, "Joe did not want to go to the party because he was feeling *all in*.") Quite a few words in English are used in idioms and these are usually given in a dictionary after the definitions of the word itself. If there are idioms for the word that you are clearing, they are cleared as well.

6. Clear any other information given about the word, such as notes on its usage, synonyms,[7] etc., so you have a full understanding of the word.

7. If you encounter[8] a misunderstood word or symbol in the definition of a word being cleared, you must clear it right away using this same procedure and then return to the definition you were clearing.

(Dictionary symbols and abbreviations are usually given in the front of the dictionary.)

However, if you find yourself spending a lot of time clearing words within definitions of words, you should get a simpler dictionary. A good dictionary will enable you to clear a word without having to look up a lot of other ones in the process.

Example of Clearing a Word

Let's say that you are reading the sentence, "He used to clean chimneys for a living," and you're not sure what *chimneys* means.

You find it in the dictionary and look through the definitions for the one that applies. It says "A flue for the smoke or gases from a fire."

You're not sure what *flue* means so you look that up. It says "A channel or passage for smoke, air or gases." That fits and makes sense, so you use it in some sentences until you have a clear concept of it.

Flue in this dictionary has other definitions, each of which you would clear and use in sentences.

Next, read the derivation the dictionary gives for the word *flue*.

---

7. **synonyms:** words in the same language that have a similar meaning to another word in that language. Example: *Big* and *large* are *synonyms*.

8. **encounter:** find oneself faced with.

Now go back to *chimney*. The definition, "A flue for the smoke or gases from a fire," now makes sense, so you use it in sentences until you have a concept of it.

You then clear the other definitions. If the dictionary you are using has specialized or obsolete definitions, you would skip them as they aren't in common usage.

Now clear up the derivation of the word. You find that *chimney* originally came from the Greek word *kaminos,* which means "furnace."

If the word had any notes about its use, synonyms or idioms, they would all be cleared too.

That would be the end of clearing *chimney*.

The above is the way a word should be cleared.

When words are understood, communication can take place, and with communication any given subject can be understood.

Drill

1. Think of or find a word you know you do not understand or are unsure of and clear it, using a dictionary.

2. Go back through the section "Handling Misunderstood Words" looking for and clearing any words you do not fully understand and re-studying the section as you go. Write up what words you found and cleared.

Simple Words

You might suppose at once that it is the BIG words or the technical words which are most misunderstood.

This is NOT the case.

On actual test, it was English simple words and NOT technical words which prevented understanding.

Words like "a," "the," "exist," "such" and other "everybody knows" words show up with great frequency as being misunderstood.

It takes a BIG dictionary to define these simple words fully. This is another oddity. The small dictionaries also suppose "everybody knows."

It is almost incredible to see that a university graduate has gone through years and years of study of complex subjects and yet[9] does not know what "or" or "by" or "an" means. It has to be seen to be believed. Yet when cleaned up, his whole education turns from a solid mass of question marks to a clean useful view.

A test of schoolchildren in Johannesburg[10] once showed that intelligence DECREASED with each new year of school!

The answer to the puzzle was simply that each year they added a few dozen more crushing[11] misunderstood words onto an already confused vocabulary that no one ever got them to look up.

Stupidity *is* the effect of misunderstood words.

In those areas which give man the most trouble, you will find the most alteration of fact, the most confused and conflicting ideas and of course the greatest number of misunderstood words. Take "economics"[12] for example.

The subject of psychology[13] began its texts by saying they did not know what the word means. So

---

9. **yet:** for all that; nevertheless; but.

---

10. **Johannesburg:** city in South Africa.

11. **crushing:** overwhelming.

12. **economics:** the science concerned with the production and consumption or use of goods and services. *See also* **science** in the glossary.

13. **psychology:** the study of the human brain and stimulus-response mechanisms. It stated that "Man, to be happy, must adjust to his environment." In other words, man, to be happy, must be a total effect. *See also* **stimulus-response** and **effect** in the glossary.

the subject itself never arrived. Professor Wundt[14] of Leipzig[15] University in 1879 perverted the term. It really means just a study *(ology)* of the soul *(psyche)*. But Wundt, working under the eye of Bismarck[16] the greatest of German military fascists,[17] at the height of German war ambitions, had to deny man had a soul. So there went the whole subject! Men were thereafter animals (it is all right to kill animals) and man had no soul, so the word psychology could no longer be defined.

THE EARLIEST MISUNDERSTOOD WORD IN A SUBJECT IS A KEY TO LATER MISUNDERSTOOD WORDS IN THAT SUBJECT.

In studying a foreign language it is often found that the grammar[18] words of one's *own* language that tell about the grammar in the foreign language are basic to *not* being able to learn the foreign language.

Not knowing the meanings of these simple words can block one's understanding of a subject. One has to look them up when they aren't understood, no matter how "simple" they may seem.

Joe did not want to go outside for it was snowing.

---

14. **Wundt:** Wilhelm Wundt (1832–1920), German psychologist and physiologist (expert in the study of the functions of living things and the ways in which their parts and organs work); the originator of the false doctrine that man is no more than an animal. *See also* **psychology.**

15. **Leipzig:** a city in Germany; the location of Leipzig University, where Wilhelm Wundt and others developed "modern" psychology. *See also* **psychology** and **Wundt.**

16. **Bismarck:** Otto von Bismarck (1815–1898), German political leader and first chancellor (chief of government) from 1871–1890. Bismarck was called the "iron chancellor"; he fought wars with Denmark, Austria and France as part of his plans to unify Germany.

17. **fascists:** people who believe in or practice *fascism,* the principles or methods of a government or a political party favoring rule by a dictator, with strong control of industry and labor by the central government, great restrictions upon the freedom of individuals, and extreme nationalism and militarism.

18. **grammar:** the way words are organized into speech and writings so as to convey exact thoughts, ideas and meanings amongst people. It is essentially a system of agreements as to the relationship of words to bring about meaningful communication.

Drill

1. Write down an example of a subject you have studied which seems complex to you. How could you go about making this subject understandable?

The Two Phenomena of Misunderstood Words

First Phenomenon

When a student misses understanding a word, the section right after that word is a blank in his memory.

You can always trace back to the word just before the blank, get it understood and find miraculously that the former blank area is not now blank in the material he is studying. The above is pure magic.

Second Phenomenon

As covered earlier, when a word is not grasped, the student then goes into a noncomprehension (blankness) of things immediately after.

This is followed by the student's solution for the blank condition which is to individuate from it— separate self from it.

Now that the student is individuated from the area, he then commits harmful acts against the more general area.

This is followed by an effort to restrain himself from committing more harmful acts and efforts to find ways he has been wronged. This is followed by various mental and physical conditions and by various complaints, faultfinding and look-what-you-did-to-me.

This justifies[19] a departure, a blow.

---

19. justifies: shows to be just or right; gives a good reason for; defends.

But most educational systems, frowning[20] on blows as they do, cause the student to really withdraw himself from whatever he was studying and set up in its place mental machinery which can receive and give back sentences and phrases.

COMPUTERS CAN...

---

20. frowning: looking with displeasure or disapproval (*on* or *upon*).

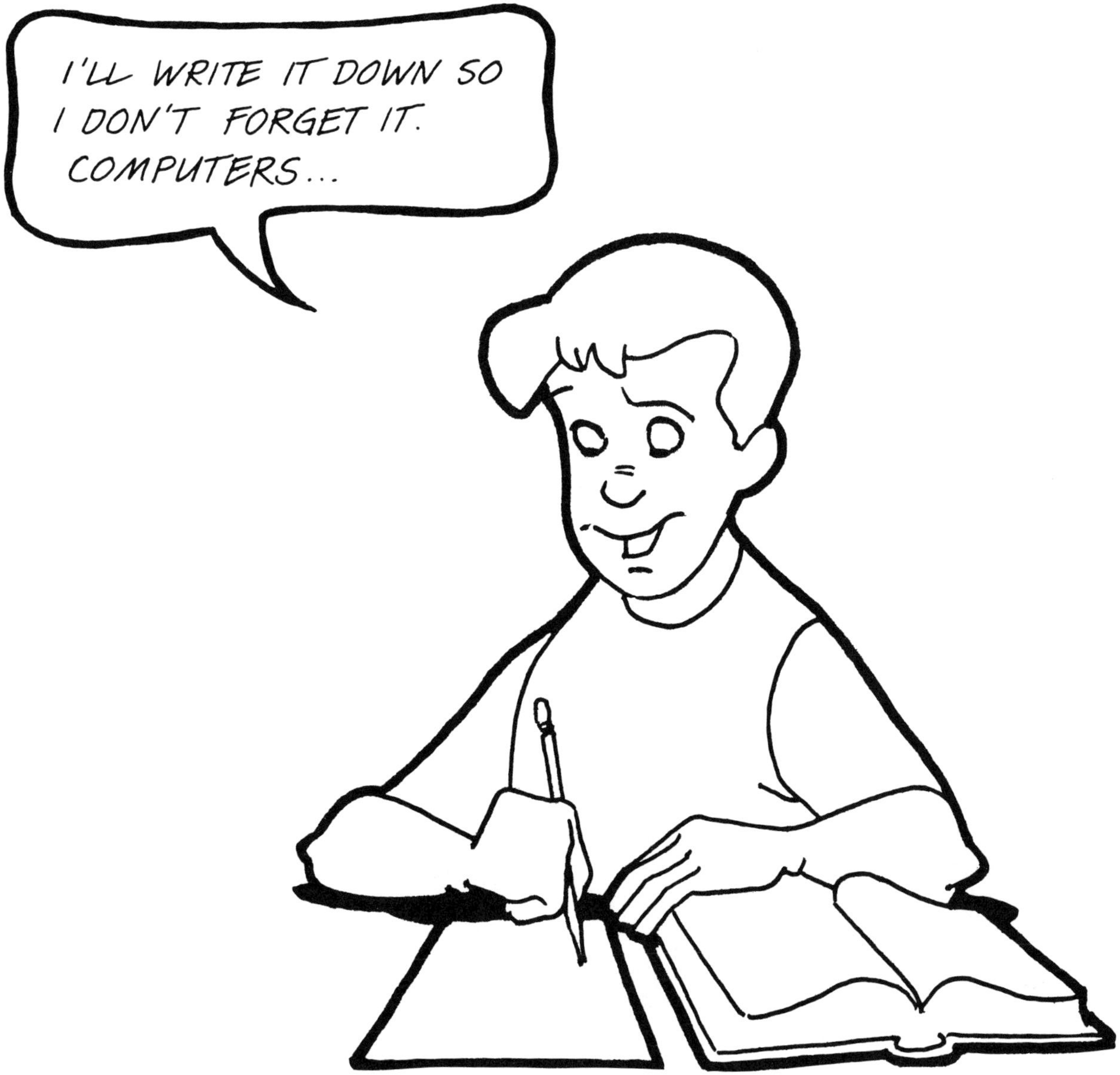
I'LL WRITE IT DOWN SO I DON'T FORGET IT. COMPUTERS...

We now have "the quick student who somehow never applies what he learns." This is known as a "glib"[21] student.

The specific phenomenon then is that a student can study some words and give them back and yet be no participant to the action. The student gets A+ on exams but can't apply the data.

---

21. **glib:** characterized by fluency (a smooth, easy flow) or readiness, but implying lack of thought or of sincerity.

The very bright student who can't yet use the data isn't there at all. He has long since ceased to confront the subject matter or the subject.

The thoroughly dull[22] student is just stuck in the noncomprehend blankness following some misunderstood word.

The cure for either of these conditions of "bright noncomprehension" or "dull" is to find the missing word.

---

22. dull: mentally slow; lacking brightness of mind; somewhat stupid.

Drill

1. Write down an example of someone you have observed who exhibited the *first* phenomenon of a misunderstood word.

2. Write down an example of someone you have observed who exhibited the *second* phenomenon of a misunderstood word.

CHAPTER FOUR:

DICTIONARIES

How to Use a Dictionary

Diction comes from the Latin word meaning *a word* or *to say*; *-ary* means *a collection of* or *a thing connected with*.

A dictionary tells a person how to say a word, what it means, how to spell it and how to use it. Dictionaries usually will tell you where a word comes from.

A dictionary is a word book.

Definitions in dictionaries are not always complete and in some cases are not totally correct. Remember that dictionaries are written by people who themselves might have misunderstoods. So do not treat them as religious texts which must be believed. They are mostly correct but they are just tools.

The Alphabet

Knowledge of the alphabet is the key to finding words quickly. To use a dictionary rapidly one has to be able to recite the alphabet rapidly and know the relations of letters in the alphabet one to the other instantly. Otherwise, one can get lost and it will take a long time to look up words. One literally has to know the alphabet backwards and forwards.

Words are arranged in alphabetical order in all dictionaries. A dictionary has a section for each letter of the alphabet. The first letter of the word one is looking up tells one which section of the dictionary to look in. Within any section, words are further arranged alphabetically by their second letters, then their third letters and so on. For instance, the word *cat* would be found after the word *castle* and before the word *catch*.

Drill

1. Look up the word *cat* in a dictionary. Write down what word comes just before it and what word comes just after it.

2. Look up the following words in a dictionary, using your knowledge of the alphabet to find them as quickly as possible:

apron	*house*	*mail*
deer	*window*	*straight*
gift	*nest*	*yesterday*

Guide Words

At the top of each page of the dictionary, there are words printed in black heavy type. They are called *guide words*. Guide words show the first and the last words printed on that page or in that column.

The page of the dictionary one wants can be found by looking at the guide words on each page. Guide words help one find the word being looked for faster.

Drill

1. Open a dictionary to any page. Write down the guide words at the top of the page.

2. Look up the word *fast* in the dictionary. Use the guide words to help you find this. Write down what guide words are at the top of the page where you found *fast*.

Pronunciation

Pronunciation means the way something is said. A dictionary tells one how to pronounce a word. The pronunciation of a word is given in the dictionary right after the word itself and is usually in parentheses.[1]

Pronunciation is shown by:

a. How the word is divided into syllables (a syllable is a word or a small part of a word which can be pronounced with a single, uninterrupted sounding of the voice).

For example, the word *elephant* contains three syllables:

el e phant

b. How the word, if it has two or more syllables, is accented (the emphasizing of one syllable of a word more than another).

el´ e phant

The accent mark tells one that the first syllable of the word is the one that is said with emphasis when pronouncing it.

c. How the individual letters in a word sound through use of a pronunciation key.[2]

el ə fənt

Dictionaries use letters and special marks to show how a word sounds. Generally, there are pronunciation keys at the bottom of each page or every other page which list out the most important letters and marks.

There is also a complete listing near the front which gives the use of every letter or mark used in that dictionary to show how to pronounce a word. By looking at the letters and/or marks in parentheses and checking the pronunciation key at the bottom of the page (or near the front of the dictionary), one learns how the word is pronounced. For instance, to learn how the first "e" of elephant is pronounced, one looks at the key and sees that it is pronounced in the same way as the "e" in the words *met* and *rest*. Pronunciation keys differ a bit from dictionary to dictionary but they are all used as described here.

---

1. **parentheses:** marks [( )] used to put additional information into a statement, a question or a definition. Example: She has the flowers (roses).

2. **key:** a thing that explains or solves something else, as a book of answers or a set of symbols for pronouncing words.

Drill

1. Find the pronunciation keys in your dictionary. Write down where you found these.

2. Use the pronunciation key to work out exactly how to pronounce *elephant,* using the pronunciation marks for this word given in the previous section.

3. Look up three words and work out how to pronounce them correctly using the pronunciation key.

Parts of Speech

Following the pronunciation, the dictionary gives an abbreviation which designates the word's *part of speech*. The parts of speech are the different things words do, such as name a person, place or thing *(noun)*, show action or state of being *(verb)*, modify or describe another word *(adjective* or *adverb)*, etc. This helps you to understand how that word is used in speech and writing.

When the plural[3] form of a word is made differently than by adding *-s* or *-es* to the singular,[4] the dictionary also includes the plural form of the word, directly after the part of speech.

For example, the entry for *mouse* in most dictionaries would look similar to this:

mouse (mows) *n.* (*pl.* **mice**)

---

3. **plural:** a form of a word which indicates more than one person, place or thing is being talked about.

4. **singular:** a form of a word which indicates one person, place or thing is being talked about.

Drill

1. Look up a word in a dictionary and write down what its part of speech is. Note whether or not its plural form is included in the entry.

2. Look up five more words in the dictionary, noting their parts of speech. Write down how you can use this information in clearing a word.

Definitions

Next comes the definition of the word. If it has more than one definition, most dictionaries number them.

Often dictionaries give examples showing the use of the word. But in clearing a word, it is not enough for the person simply to read these examples. He has to make up several of his own before he really knows the word.

Dictionaries also often give specialized definitions when the word has a special meaning in such subjects as law, sports, science, music and so on. They often give slang (words or phrases that are not considered to be "standard" in the language) definitions for words.

Idioms

An idiom is a phrase or expression that has a meaning different from what the words suggest in their usual meaning. For example, *to catch one's eye* is an idiom which means *to get one's attention.*

Most dictionaries include the idioms of a word after the definitions.

Drill

1. Look up the word *move* in a dictionary. Write down how many definitions it has. Write down what types of specialized definitions are given in the dictionary for this word. Write down how many idioms are given for this word. Write down how many slang definitions are included in the entry for this word.

2. Look up 5 more words in the dictionary, noting how many definitions of different types are given for each of these words.

Derivation

A word's derivation (a statement of the origin of a word) is put in brackets.[5] The derivation can be very important to one's full understanding of the word. Words get altered through the ages. By seeing the derivation one can find out what the word originally meant. The word's derivation is usually found at the beginning or the end of the definitions in the dictionary.

In the derivation certain signs and abbreviations are used.

The sign < means *derived*[6] *from.*

The sign + means *and.*

The word or words it comes from are written in italics.[7] Usually abbreviations are used to show the language the word comes from. For example, OE would mean Old English, which denotes[8] the English spoken up to approximately the twelfth century. These abbreviations are defined in the dictionary. Sometimes at the end of the derivation there is a word written in capital letters. This means that further data on the origin of the word can be found under the derivation of the word in capitals.

---

5. **brackets:** marks ([ ]) used in dictionaries:
a. to enclose additional information or directions, etc. Example: She said "I wuv [love] you."
b. sometimes to enclose examples given in the dictionary. Example: *house* 1. a building in which people live [*They are in their house.*]
c. to enclose the derivation of a word. Example: *pen* [from Old French *penne,* from Latin *penna,* feather]. *See also* **derivation** in the glossary.

6. **derived:** came from a source or origin; originated.

7. **italics:** letters that slant to the right. *These are italics.*
8. **denotes:** is a mark or sign of; indicates.

Example of a Word Entry

cool (kōol), *adj.*

1. mildly cold; neither warm nor very cold; pleasantly cold:
a cool day.

2. giving a feeling of coolness:
a cool dress.

3. calm; not excited:
to remain cool in spite of trouble.

4. *US Slang.* first rate; superior; admirable:
He drew a cool cartoon.

cool off 1. to calm down. 2. to lose interest.

[Old English *col,* related to COLD]

ōo as in boot

Drill

1. Using the sample dictionary entry shown on page 125, name each of the parts of a word entry based on what you have learned in this chapter.

Dictionary Tips

How to Break Up a Word

Occasionally, one cannot find a specific word in the dictionary, but by separating a word into its component[9] parts one can look up each part and gain its meaning. Take, for example, the word *anti-tax*. This word is not defined in most dictionaries, but one can still determine its meaning. One looks up the first part, *anti-,* and finds that it means *opposed to.* One then looks up the second part of the word, *tax,* and finds that it means *money regularly collected from citizens by their rulers.* When one combines the two parts, one gets the definition of *antitax* which means *opposed to collecting of money from citizens by their rulers.*

Dictionaries sometimes contain lists of such words which are not defined but which can be broken down into their component parts and the meaning determined.

Technical Words

Words of a special technology require a dictionary composed of terms for that field, e.g.,[10] a photographic dictionary or a nautical[11] dictionary.

To clear a foreign word, get a dictionary of that language. There are two kinds of foreign language dictionaries. One is a dictionary entirely in the foreign language. The other is half in the language the person speaks and half in the foreign language. For instance, in an English/Swedish dictionary, half of the dictionary is English with Swedish words next to it, and the other half is Swedish with its English counterpart[12] next to it. One would use the all-foreign dictionary only when the person being word cleared knew that language fluently.[13]

Dictionaries contain a lot of information. This chapter covers the basics of how to use one. The format of individual dictionaries varies one to the next but the above fundamentals apply to them all. Dictionaries contain sections in the front which explain how they are used. If one encounters a word, symbol or abbreviation in the entry of a word that he does not understand he can always turn to this introductory section for help.

---

9. **component:** serving as one of the elements or ingredients of a whole.

10. **e.g.:** for example; from the Latin words *exempli gratia.*

11. **nautical:** of sailors or seamanship.

12. **counterpart:** a person or thing closely resembling another, especially in function.

13. **fluently:** so as to be able to write or speak easily, smoothly and expressively.

Drill

1. Look for the word *nonbeliever* in a dictionary. Note that this word has no entry. Now look up the two parts, *non-* and *believer* and work out what the word means. (On the page which defines *non-*, note the list of words which start with *non-* but are not included as their own entries.) Write down the definition you worked out for *nonbeliever*.

2. Write down an example of a subject you know of which has its own specialized dictionary.

3. Look in the front of your dictionary and locate the section which explains how that dictionary is organized and used.

Recommended Dictionaries

Dictionaries are vital and important tools in studying or learning any subject. However, current dictionaries vary in accuracy and usefulness and many of these modern dictionaries are virtually[14] useless and can actually confuse a student due to their false and omitted definitions and grammatical errors. So the dictionary that a student chooses to use is important and can actually make a difference in his success as a student.

As dictionaries are such an important factor in the learning and application of any subject, a list of some dictionaries that have been found to be the best of those currently available is included here.

Webster's New World Dictionary for Young Readers:

This is a very simple American dictionary. It is available in most bookstores and is published by New World Dictionaries/Simon & Schuster. It is a hardbound volume and does not contain derivations. When using this dictionary, a student must be sure to clear the derivations in a larger dictionary. The definitions in this dictionary are quite good.

Oxford American Dictionary:

This is a very good American dictionary, simpler than the college dictionaries yet more advanced than the beginning dictionary listed above. It does not list derivations of the words. It is quite an excellent dictionary and very popular with students who want to use an intermediate dictionary.

It is published in paperback by Avon Books and in hardback by Oxford University Press.

Webster's New World Dictionary of the American Language, Student Edition:

This is an intermediate-level American dictionary which includes derivations. It is published by New World Dictionaries/Simon & Schuster and is available in most bookstores.

---

14. **virtually:** for the most part; almost wholly; just about.

The Random House College Dictionary:

This is a college dictionary and somewhat of a higher gradient than the dictionaries listed above. This is a one-volume American dictionary published in the US by Random House, Inc., and in Canada by Random House of Canada, Limited.

This Random House dictionary contains a large number of slang definitions and idioms and also gives good derivations.

The Webster's New World Dictionary of the American Language, College Edition:

This is an American college dictionary published by New World Dictionaries/Simon & Schuster. It is a one-volume dictionary and gives most of the slang definitions and idioms. It also has good derivations.

The Concise[15] Oxford Dictionary:

This is a very concise English dictionary but is not a simple or beginner's dictionary. It is a small, one-volume dictionary. It uses a lot of abbreviations which may take some getting used to, but once the abbreviations are mastered students find this dictionary as easy to use as any other similarly advanced dictionary. It is less complicated in its definitions than the usual college dictionary and has the added benefit that the definitions given are well stated—in other words, it does not give the same definition reworded into several different definitions, the way some dictionaries do.

This dictionary is printed in Great Britain and the United States by the Oxford University Press.

The Shorter Oxford English Dictionary:

This is a two-volume English dictionary and is a shorter version of *The Oxford English Dictionary*. It is quite up-to-date and is an ideal dictionary for fairly literate[16] students. Even if not used regularly, it makes a very good reference dictionary. The definitions given in the Oxford dictionaries are usually more accurate and give a better idea of the meaning of the word than any other dictionary.

This Oxford dictionary is also printed by the Oxford University Press.

---

15. **concise:** brief and to the point; short and clear.

16. **literate:** knowledgeable; educated.

The Oxford English Dictionary:

This is by far the largest English dictionary and is actually the principal[17] dictionary of the English language. It consists of twenty volumes. (There is a *Compact Edition of the Oxford English Dictionary* in which the exact text of *The Oxford English Dictionary* is duplicated in very small print which is read through a magnifying glass. Reduced in this manner the whole thing fits into two volumes.)

For many students this dictionary may be too comprehensive[18] to use on a regular basis. (For some students huge dictionaries can be confusing as the words they use in their definitions are often too big or too rare and make one chase[19] through twenty new words to get the meaning of the original.)

Although many students will not use this as their only dictionary, it is a must for every classroom and will be found useful in clearing certain words, verifying data from other dictionaries, etc. It is a valuable reference dictionary and is sometimes the only dictionary that correctly defines a particular word.

These Oxfords are also printed by the Oxford University Press. If your local bookstore does not stock[20] them, they will be able to order them for you.

From the dictionaries recommended here, a student should be able to find one that suits[21] him. Whatever dictionary one chooses, it should be the correct gradient for him. For instance, you wouldn't give a foreign language student, who barely knows English, the big *Oxford English Dictionary* to use in his studies!

Dinky Dictionaries

"Dinky[22] dictionaries" are the kind you can fit in your pocket. They are usually paperback and sold at magazine counters in drugstores and grocery stores.

In learning the meaning of words, small dictionaries are very often a greater liability than they are a help.

---

17. **principal:** first in rank, authority, importance, etc.; chief; main.
18. **comprehensive:** including much.
19. **chase:** go in pursuit; follow along.

20. **stock:** get or keep a supply of, as for sale or for future use.
21. **suits:** satisfies; meets the demands or needs of.
22. **dinky:** *(informal)* small, insignificant.

The meanings they give are often circular: Like "CAT: An Animal." "ANIMAL: A Cat." They do not give enough meaning to escape the circle.

The meanings given are often inadequate to get a real concept of the word.

The words are too few and even common words are often missing.

Little pocketbook dictionaries may have their uses for traveling and reading newspapers, but they do get people in trouble. People have been seen to find a word in them and then look around in total confusion. For the dinky dictionary did not give the full meaning or the second meaning they really needed.

So the dinky dictionary may fit in your pocket but not in your mind.

Don't use a dinky dictionary.

Dictionaries and a Person's Own Language

English dictionaries and American dictionaries differ in some of their definitions, as the Americans (USA) and English (Britain) define some words differently.

An English dictionary will have different applications[23] of words that are specifically *English* (British). These usages won't necessarily be found in American dictionaries, as they are not part of the *American* English language. Different dictionaries have things in them which are unique[24] to that language.

The Oxford English Dictionary is a good example of an English dictionary for the English.

For the most part a student's dictionary should correspond to his own language. This does not mean that an American shouldn't use a British dictionary (or vice versa), but if he does, he should be aware of the above and check words in a dictionary of his own language as needed.

---

23. applications: ways of applying or methods of applying or using; specific uses.

24. unique: limited in occurrence to a given class, situation or area.

False and Omitted Definitions

It has been found that some dictionaries leave out definitions and may even contain false definitions. If, when using a dictionary, a student comes across what he suspects to be a false definition, there is a handling that can be done. The first thing would be to ensure there are no misunderstoods in the definition in question and then he should consult[25] another dictionary and check its definition for the word being cleared. This may require more than one dictionary. In this way any false definitions can be resolved.

Other dictionaries, encyclopedias[26] and textbooks should be on hand for reference.

If a student runs into an omitted definition or a suspected omitted definition, then other dictionaries or reference books should be consulted and the omitted definition found and cleared.

Derivations

A derivation is a statement of the origin of a word.

Words *originated* somewhere and meant something originally. Through the ages they have sometimes become altered in meaning.

Derivations are important in getting a full understanding of words. By understanding the origin of a word, one will have a far greater grasp of the concept of that word. Students find that they are greatly assisted in understanding a word fully and conceptually if they know the word's derivation.

A student must always clear the derivation of any word he looks up.

It will commonly be found that a student does not know how to read the derivations of the words in most dictionaries. The most common error they make is not understanding that when there is a word in the derivation which is fully capitalized it means that that word appears elsewhere in the dictionary and probably contains more information

---

25. **consult:** seek information or advice from; refer to.

26. **encyclopedias:** a book or set of books giving information on all or many branches of knowledge, or on one field of study, generally in articles alphabetically arranged.

about the derivation. (For example, the derivation of "thermometer" is given in one dictionary as THERMO + METER. Looking at the derivation of "thermo," it says it is from the Greek word *therme,* meaning *heat.* And the derivation of "meter" is given as coming from the French *metre,* which is from the Latin "metrum," which is itself from the Greek *metron* meaning *measure.*) By understanding and using these fully capitalized words, a student can get a full picture of a word's derivation.

If a student has trouble with derivations, it is most likely because of the above plus a misunderstood word or symbol in the derivation. These points can be cleared up quite easily where they are giving difficulty.

An excellent dictionary of derivations is *The Oxford Dictionary of English Etymology,*[27] also printed by the Oxford University Press.

We have long known the importance of clearing words and it stands to reason that the dictionary one uses to do this would also be quite important.

---

27. **etymology:** an account of the origin and development of a word and its meaning.

Drill

1. Go through several dictionaries and locate the one that is best for you. Refer to the list of recommended dictionaries in the section you have just read. Write down which dictionary you found to be the best one for you.

CHAPTER FIVE:

DEMONSTRATION

The Use of Demonstration

The word *demonstration* means to show, or to show how something works. It comes from the Latin word *demonstrare,* to point out, show, prove.

In studying, a student can do a "demonstration" or "demo" with a "demo kit" which consists of various small objects such as corks, caps, paper clips, pen tops, rubber bands, etc. The student demonstrates an idea or principle with his hands and the pieces of his demo kit.

If a student ran into something he couldn't quite figure out, a demo kit would assist him to understand it. By making the different pieces of the demo kit represent the objects he is studying about, the student can move them around and see more clearly how they relate to each other, etc.

By doing this the student is getting mass to go along with the ideas studied.

Drill

1. Assemble a demo kit for your own use.

2. Using your demo kit, demonstrate a principle you are familiar with. Write down what you did and what you learned in doing this.

Clay Table Training

Another form of demonstration is using clay figures to demonstrate a concept or principle. This is called clay table training. The purpose of clay table training is:

1. To make the materials being studied real to the student by making him DEMONSTRATE them in clay.

2. To give a proper balance of mass and significance.[1]

3. To teach the student to *apply*.

The student is given a word or situation to demonstrate. He does this in clay, labeling each part. The clay SHOWS the thing. It is *not* just a blob of clay with a label on it. Use small strips of paper for labels. The whole demonstration then has a label of what it is.

When the student has completed his clay demonstration it is then examined by the Supervisor[2] or another student. Before the checkout,[3] the student removes the overall label. The student must be silent. The examiner must not ask any questions.

The examiner just looks and figures out what it is. He then tells the student who then shows the examiner the label. If the examiner did not see what it was, it is a flunk.[4]

Clay table must not be reduced to significance by the student explaining or answering questions. Nor is it reduced to significance by long-winded[5] labels of individual parts. The clay *shows* it, not the label.

The clay demonstrates it. The student must learn the difference between mass and significance.

---

1. **significance:** any thought, decision, concept, idea, purpose or meaning connected with something as opposed to its mass. *See also* **mass** in the glossary.

2. **Supervisor:** the person in charge of a course and its students. The job of the Supervisor is to ensure that his students duplicate, understand and apply the materials of the course being studied. *See also* **duplication** in the glossary.

3. **checkout:** the action of verifying a student's knowledge of what he has studied.

4. **flunk:** failure on a course or examination or checkout. *See also* **checkout.**

5. **long-winded:** speaking or writing at great, often tiresome length.

For example, the student has to demonstrate a pencil. He makes a thin roll of clay which is surrounded by another layer of clay—the thin roll sticking slightly out of one end. On the other end goes a small cylinder[6] of clay. The roll is labeled "lead." The outer layer is labeled "wood." The small cylinder is labeled "rubber." Then a label is made for the whole thing: "pencil."

On checkout, the student removes "pencil" before the examiner can see it. If the examiner can look at it and say "It's a pencil," the student passes.

---

6. cylinder: a solid or hollow object with straight sides and circular ends.

Clay Demo Size

Clay demos must be large.

One of the purposes of clay table training is to make the materials being studied *real* to the student. If a student's clay demo is small (less mass), the reality factor may not be sufficient. And long experience has shown that BIG clay demos are more successful in terms of increasing student understanding.

ART is no object in clay table work. The forms are crude.[7]

Labeling Clay Demonstrations

Each separate thing is labeled that is made on the clay table, no matter how crude the label is. Students usually do labels with scraps of paper written on with a ballpoint. When cutting out a label, a point is put on one end, making it easy to stick the label into the clay.

The procedure should go—student makes one object, labels it, makes another object, labels it, makes a third object and puts a label on it and so on in sequence. This comes from the data that optimum[8] learning requires an equal balance of mass and significance and that too much of one without the other can make the student feel bad. If a student makes all the masses of his demonstration at once, without labeling them, he is sitting there with all those significances stacking up in his mind instead of putting down each one (in the form of a label) as he goes. The correct procedure is *label each mass as you go along.*

---

7. **crude:** not carefully made or done; rough.

8. **optimum:** most favorable or desirable; best.

Representing Thoughts in Clay

Any thought can be represented by a piece of clay and a label. The mass parts are done by clay, the significance or thought parts by label.

A thin-edged ring of clay with a large hole in it is usually used to signify a pure significance.

Directions of flows or travel are usually indicated with little arrows and this can become important. The arrow can be made out of clay or it can be made as another type of label. It is often lack of data in the demo about which way what is going or which way what is flowing that makes the demo unrecognizable.

Working Things Out in Clay

Anything can be demonstrated in clay if you work at it. And just by working on *how* to demonstrate it or make it into clay and labels brings about renewed understanding.

In the phrase "how do I represent it in clay" is contained the secret of teaching. If one can represent it in clay, one understands it. If one can't, one really doesn't understand what it is. So clay and labels work only if the term or things are truly understood. And working them out in clay brings about an understanding of them.

A well-done clay demo, which actually does demonstrate, will produce a marvelous change in the student. And he will retain the data.

Sketching

Sketching is also part of demonstration and part of working things out.

Someone sitting at his office desk trying to work something out doesn't have any clay to hand to work it out with, but he could work it out with a little demo kit action or a paper and pencil, draw graphs of it, and so forth. This is a necessary part of getting a grip on something.

There is a rule which goes IF YOU CANNOT DEMONSTRATE SOMETHING IN TWO DIMENSIONS[9] YOU HAVE IT WRONG. It's an arbitrary[10] rule, but it's very workable.

This rule is used in engineering[11] and architecture.[12] If it can't be worked out simply and clearly in two dimensions, there is something wrong and it couldn't be built.

It works in other ways too.

---

9. **dimensions:** any measurable extents, as length, width, depth, etc. Something which is in two dimensions would have the dimensions of height and width only; in other words, it would be flat.

10. **arbitrary:** derived only from opinion or preference; not based on the nature of things.

11. **engineering:** the planning, designing, construction or management of machinery, roads, bridges, buildings, waterways, etc.

12. **architecture:** the science, art or profession of designing and constructing buildings, bridges, etc. *See also* **science** in the glossary.

An obvious example is a navigator[13] who, instead of trying to work it all out in his head with some foggy[14] concept of where he is, simply graphs the sailing plan and progress on a chart.

This is all part of demonstration and part of working something out.

---

13. **navigator:** a person who directs the course of (a ship or aircraft or vehicle, etc.).

14. **foggy:** not clear; dim; blurred.

Drill

1. Use sketching to do a demonstration of a student clearing a misunderstood word.

CHAPTER SIX:

WORD CLEARING

Methods of Word Clearing

There are several methods for locating and handling misunderstood words. Three of the most commonly used methods are fully described in this chapter.

Method 3 Word Clearing

A student must know how to keep himself tearing[1] along successfully in his studies. He should be able to handle anything that slows or interferes with his progress. He applies the study technology to assist himself.

A student who uses study technology will look up each word he comes to that he doesn't understand and will never leave a word behind him that he doesn't know the meaning of.

If he runs into trouble, the student himself, the Supervisor, or his study partner uses a method of Word Clearing called Method 3 Word Clearing to handle anything that slowed or interfered with his progress.

Waiting to get groggy[2] or to "dope off"[3] as the only detection of misunderstoods and handling it is waiting too long. As soon as the student slows down or he isn't quite so "bright" as he was fifteen minutes ago is the time to look for the misunderstood word. It's not a misunderstood phrase or idea or concept but a misunderstood WORD. This always occurs before the subject itself is not understood.

---

1. **tearing:** moving very quickly.

---

2. **groggy:** shaky or dizzy, as from a blow, lack of sleep, etc.
3. **dope off:** get tired, sleepy, foggy (as though *doped,* or drugged).

Method 3 Word Clearing is done as follows:

1. The student is not flying[4] along and is not so "bright" as he was or he may exhibit[5] just plain lack of enthusiasm or be taking too long on the course or be yawning or disinterested or doodling[6] or daydreaming, etc.

---

4. **flying:** moving or going swiftly.

5. **exhibit:** show; display.

6. **doodling:** scribbling or drawing aimlessly, especially when one's attention is elsewhere.

2. The student must then look earlier in the text for a misunderstood word. There is one always; there are no exceptions. It may be that the misunderstood word is two pages or more back, but it is always earlier in the text than where the student is now.

3. The word is found. The student recognizes it in looking back for it. Or, if the student can't find it, one can take words from the text that could be the misunderstood word and ask, "What does ____ mean?" to see if the student gives the correct definition.

4. The student looks up the word found in a dictionary and clears it per the steps of clearing a misunderstood word. He uses it verbally several times in sentences of his own composition until he has obviously demonstrated he understands the word by the composition of his sentences.

5. The student now reads the text that contained the misunderstood word. If he is not now "bright," eager to get on with it, feeling happier, etc., then there is another misunderstood word earlier in the text. This is found by repeating steps 2–5.

6. When the student is bright, feeling happier, etc., he comes forward, studying the text from where the misunderstood word was to the area of the subject he did not understand (where step 1 began).

The student will now be enthusiastic with his study of the subject, and that is the end result of Method 3 Word Clearing. (The result won't be achieved if a misunderstood word was missed or if there is an earlier misunderstood word in the text. If so, repeat steps 2–5.) If the student is now enthusiastic, have him continue with studying.

Good Word Clearing is a system of backtracking. You have to look earlier than the point where the student became dull or confused and you'll find that there's a word that he doesn't understand somewhere before the trouble started. If he doesn't brighten up when the word is found and cleared, there will be a misunderstood word even before that one.

This will be very clear to you if you understand that IF IT IS NOT RESOLVING, THE THING THE STUDENT IS APPARENTLY HAVING TROUBLE WITH IS NOT THE THING THE STUDENT IS HAVING TROUBLE WITH. Otherwise, it would resolve, wouldn't it? If he knew what he didn't understand, he could resolve it himself. So to talk to him about what he thinks he doesn't understand just gets nowhere. The trouble is earlier.

Zeroing In on the Word

The formula is to find out where the student wasn't having any trouble and find out where the student is now having trouble and the misunderstood word will be in between. It will be at the tag end[7] of where he wasn't having trouble.

Method 3 Word Clearing is tremendously effective when done as described herein.[8] So get a good reality on it and become expert in its use.

---

7. **tag end:** the last or final part of something.

8. **herein:** in this writing.

Drill

1. Write down *when* you would use Method 3 Word Clearing on yourself or on another.

2. Using your demo kit, demonstrate how to do each of the steps of Method 3 Word Clearing.

Method 9 Word Clearing

Method 9 Word Clearing is a way of finding the words a person doesn't understand in a book or other written material by having him read it aloud to the Word Clearer (person who is applying the Word Clearing technology to another). It is done on a turnabout basis (one student is the Word Clearer and word clears the other student, and then they switch around and the student who was just word cleared becomes the Word Clearer and word clears his partner).

The student and Word Clearer sit across from each other at a table.

Each has his own copy of the text to be word cleared. The Word Clearer must be able to see the student and the page in front of him at the same time.

A good, simple English dictionary and any other dictionaries the student may need are available. Any encyclopedias or texts that might be needed should also be on hand.

STUDENT   WORD CLEARER

The Word Clearer tells the student that if he reads anything he doesn't fully understand he should tell the Word Clearer, or if he sees a word he doesn't know the meaning of, he should stop and look the word up and clear it instead of going past it.

The student reads the text aloud to the Word Clearer.

As the student reads, the Word Clearer follows the text, watches the student and listens to the student.

If the student errs[9] or stumbles[10] in any way in reading, or does anything wrong or does anything odd,

---

9. **errs:** makes a mistake; is incorrect.

10. **stumbles:** speaks, acts, etc., in a clumsy or hesitating way.

. . . or does anything except comfortably and easily
read the text with understanding,

. . . the Word Clearer and student must locate the exact misunderstood word or symbol. It will usually be found *before* (and only occasionally *at*) the point the nonoptimum reaction occurred.

(The student may be able to spot his misunderstood word right away and tell the Word Clearer what it is.)

IS THERE SOME WORD OR SYMBOL THERE THAT YOU DIDN'T UNDERSTAND?

Once the misunderstood is found it must be fully cleared in the dictionary.

The student looks rapidly over the definitions to find the one which applies to the text where the word was misunderstood.

The student reads the definition aloud to the Word Clearer.

When the student understands the definition itself, he tells the Word Clearer, *in his own words,* what the definition means.

The student makes up sentences using the word correctly until he is very comfortable using the word. The sentences must show he knows how to use the word in the sense of the definition he's just cleared. The student may need to make up ten sentences, or even more, before he really understands the word and how to use it.

He does this with each definition of the word.

(He doesn't clear specialized, obsolete or archaic definitions unless the word is being used that way in the text where it was misunderstood.)

The student clears the derivation of the word.

(The student clears any idioms in the same way that he cleared the definitions. He then clears any usage notes or data on synonyms which is given and makes sure he understands them.)

Then he rereads that sentence.

If it is not obvious to the student there was a non-optimum reaction and he just continues reading, the Word Clearer stops him and asks him if there is some word or symbol there that he didn't understand.

If he has difficulty finding the misunderstood word or symbol the Word Clearer helps him find it.

The Word Clearer helps him by getting him to look earlier and earlier in the text from the point where he reacted until the misunderstood word is found.

The Word Clearer can also choose words from the text the student has already read and check with him to see if he knows the definitions.

If the student is uncertain about any words or gives a wrong definition, then that word is taken up and cleared in the dictionary.

He first clears the definition that fits.

But maybe he doesn't understand a word in the definition.

He then clears that word.

Once the misunderstood word in the definition is cleared, he goes back to the word he was clearing before. He rereads the definition he was on and finishes clearing the word.

brown: 1 a color between orange and black . . .

Then he rereads the sentence and continues.

And so it goes.

Any discomfort, nonoptimum conduct, mishandling, unsmoothness, tension, robotness[11] is checked into by the Word Clearer.

THE QUICK BROWN FOX JUMPED OVER THE LAZY FENCE.

THAT'S IT. IS THERE SOME WORD OR SYMBOL THERE THAT YOU DIDN'T UNDERSTAND?

---

11. robotness: state, quality or instance of being a robot, a person who acts or works in an automatic or mechanical way.

Is it the word he just said, or a word or symbol
before it?

When a section of the text has been word cleared in this way and the student understands it,

. . . they switch around and the student who just completed being word cleared becomes the Word Clearer.

WORD CLEARER   STUDENT

The student goes through the same section of text and then goes on to the next fresh passage.

They take it in turns like this, word clearing it section by section until they have both finished the whole text.

During the Word Clearing session, the Word Clearer should keep a record (worksheet) of the words looked up and cleared and any other important information concerning the Word Clearing.

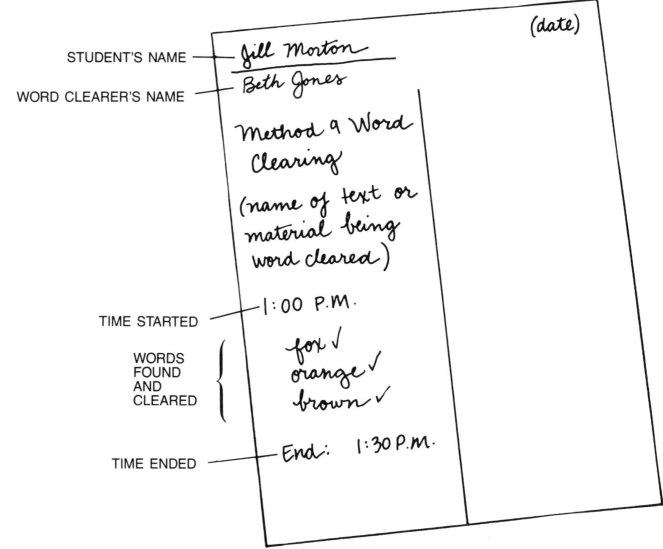

STUDENT'S NAME —— *Jill Morton*

WORD CLEARER'S NAME —— *Beth Jones*

Method 9 Word Clearing

(name of text or material being word cleared)

TIME STARTED —— *1:00 P.M.*

WORDS FOUND AND CLEARED { *fox* ✓
orange ✓
brown ✓

TIME ENDED —— *End: 1:30 P.M.*

(date)

Drill

1. Using your demo kit, demonstrate how to do each step of Method 9 Word Clearing.

2. Find another student or a friend to do this drill with. In this drill, one of you will be Student A and one of you will be Student B. Decide who is going to be Student A and who is going to be Student B.

a. Student A (as Word Clearer) Method 9 word clears Student B on the following paragraph. Use a simple dictionary.

The quick brown fox jumped over the lazy dog. The dog was supposed to be guarding the chickens but had gone to sleep. The fox sneaked into the chicken coop without anyone noticing.

b. Student B (as Word Clearer) Method 9 word clears Student A on the following paragraphs.

The quick brown fox jumped over the lazy dog. The dog was supposed to be guarding the chickens but had gone to sleep. The fox sneaked into the chicken coop without anyone noticing.

As soon as the chickens noticed him they all made a dreadful row. The fox had to move very quickly; he grabbed hold of the nearest chicken by her neck and slunk off out of the coop.

c. Student A (as Word Clearer) Method 9 word clears Student B on the following paragraphs. Use a simple dictionary.

As soon as the chickens noticed him they all made a dreadful row. The fox had to move very quickly; he grabbed hold of the nearest chicken by her neck and slunk off out of the coop.

The farmer's wife came running out of the house when she heard the din, wondering what could possibly be going on with her chickens. She saw the fox disappearing into the nearby woods with the chicken.

d. Student B (as Word Clearer) Method 9 word clears Student A on the following paragraphs.

The farmer's wife came running out of the house when she heard the din, wondering what could possibly be going on with her chickens. She saw the fox disappearing into the nearby woods with the chicken.

She shrieked loudly and looked around for the dog whose prime duty it was to prevent this sort of occurrence. The dog looked quite abashed. The farmer's wife spent the next few minutes violently upbraiding him for his apathetic behavior.

e. Student A (as Word Clearer) Method 9 word clears Student B on the following paragraph. Use a simple dictionary.

She shrieked loudly and looked around for the dog whose prime duty it was to prevent this sort of occurrence. The dog looked quite abashed. The farmer's wife spent the next few minutes violently upbraiding him for his apathetic behavior.

3. Write down what you learned in doing the previous drill, and how you can use Method 9 Word Clearing in your own life.

Method 7 Word Clearing

Whenever one is working with children or foreign language persons or semiliterates,[12] a method of Word Clearing called METHOD 7 or READING ALOUD is used.

In this method the person is made to read *aloud* to find out what he is doing.

It is a very simple method.

It is used on such persons before other Word Clearing methods in order to get the person untangled.

If a person does not seem to be progressing by studying silently, one has him read aloud.

Another copy of the same text must also be followed by the Word Clearer as the person reads.

Startling things can be observed.

The person may omit the word "is" whenever it occurs. The person doesn't read it. He may have some strange meaning for it like "Israel" (actual occurrence).

He may omit "didn't" each time it occurs and the reason may trace to not knowing what the apostrophe[13] is (actual occurrence).

He may call one word quite another word such as "stop" for "happen" or "green" for "mean."

He may hesitate[14] over certain words.

---

12. **semiliterates:** people who are barely able to read and write.

13. **apostrophe:** a mark (') used to show that a letter or letters have been left out of a word (Example: can't [cannot]), or that something is owned (Example: Joe's bicycle).

14. **hesitate:** pause; stop momentarily.

The procedure is:

1. Have him read aloud.

2. Note each omission[15] or word change or hesitation or frown as he reads and take it up at once.

---

15. omission: anything which one failed to include; anything left out.

3. Correct it by looking it up for him or explaining it to him.

4. Have him go on reading, noting the next omission, word change or hesitation or frown.

5. Repeat steps 2 to 4.

By doing this a person can be brought up to literacy.

His next actions would be learning how to use a dictionary and look up words.

Then a simple grammar text.[*]

A very backward student can be boosted[16] up to literacy by this method.

16. **boosted:** pushed upward.

Drill

1. Using your demo kit, demonstrate how to do each step of Method 7 Word Clearing.

2. Find another student or a friend to act as the person being word cleared, and drill doing Method 7 Word Clearing. Use a simple book or magazine as the text being word cleared. Continue the drill until you can easily do the steps of Method 7 Word Clearing and you feel confident that you can apply this data.

CHAPTER SEVEN:

COACHING AND CHECKOUTS

Coaching

Coaching is a vital part of study technology.

It is used frequently in doing drills on specific actions. In coaching drills, two students work together, one acting as a trainer to help the other achieve the purpose of the drill. Once the first student has become competent on the action, he becomes the coach to help the other student through.

Coaching can also be used in theory, when a student is having a hard time studying something. Coaching theory means getting a student to define *all* the words, give *all* the rules, demonstrate things in his materials with his hands or bits of things, and also may include doing clay demos.

Any student who is having any trouble or is slow or glib should team up with another student of comparable difficulties with whom he can do theory coaching.

Drill

1. Using your demo kit, demonstrate how to do theory coaching with another student.

2. Find another student or a friend to work with you, and drill doing theory coaching on some textbook or subject. Write down what you did and how you can use the data on theory coaching in your own studies.

Checkouts

A *checkout* is the action of verifying a student's knowledge of what he has studied. A checkout is *not* a test of whether or not the student can memorize what he has read.

It will never do a student any good at all to know some facts. The student is expected only to *use* facts.

Giving a checkout on the material a student has studied by seeing if it can be quoted or paraphrased[1] proves exactly nothing. This will not guarantee that the student knows the data or can use or apply it nor even guarantees that the student is there. Neither the "bright" student nor the "dull" student (both suffering from the same malady[2]) will benefit from such an examination.

So examining by seeing if somebody "knows" the text and can quote or paraphrase it is completely false and *must not be done*.

Correct examination is done only by making the person being tested answer:

a. The meanings of the words (redefining the words used in his own words and demonstrating their use in his own made-up sentences), and

b. Demonstrating how the data is *used*.

"What is the first paragraph?" is about as dull as one can get. "What are the rules given about _____?" is a question one should never bother to ask. Neither of these tell the examiner whether he has the bright nonapplier or the dull student before him. Such questions just beg for the student's criticism and course blows.

Example of How to Do a Checkout

I would go over the first paragraph of any material I was examining a student on and pick out a few uncommon words. I'd ask the student to define each and demonstrate its use in a made-up sentence and flunk the first "well . . . er . . . let me see . . . " and that would be the end of that checkout.

Above all, I myself would be sure I knew what the words meant before I started to examine.

When the student had the words, I'd demand the music. What tune do these words play?

---

1. **paraphrased:** expressed (something spoken or written) by putting it into different words having the same meaning.

2. **malady:** a disease; illness; sickness: often used figuratively.

I'd say, "All right, what use is this text assign-
ment to you?" Questions like, "Now this rule here
about not letting people eat candy while dieting, how
come there'd be such a rule?" If the student couldn't
imagine why, I'd send him back to the words just
ahead of that rule to find the one he hadn't grasped.

But if the student weren't up to the point of
study where knowing *why* he used that rule was
part of his materials, I wouldn't ask. It is very important that a student not be examined above his or
her level.

How to Do Theory Checkouts

Before any person gives another a checkout, he must himself have read or listened to the material. This will make it possible to consult the understanding and the ability to apply the material of the person being checked out.

The important points of a text are:

1. The specific rules, axioms,[3] or maxims;[4]

2. The doingness details, exactly how it is done;

and

3. The theory of why it is done.

All else (except of course, that the student knows what the words mean) is unnecessary. All you have to demand is the above.

1. The rules, laws, theories, axioms and maxims *must* be known and the student must be able to *show* their meaning is also known to him or her.

2. The doingness must be exactly known as to sequence and actions but not verbatim (in the same words as the text).

3. The theory must be known as a line of reasoning, reasons why or related data and with accuracy, but not verbatim.

The date of the book, lecture, or manual is relatively unimportant, and other details of like nature[5] should never be asked for.

If a student is ever going to apply the data, then above (1) must be down cold, (2) must be able to be experienced and (3) must be appreciated.

Asking for anything else is to rebuff[6] interest and give a feeling of failure to the person being examined.

---

3. **axioms:** established principles or laws of a science, art, etc. *See also* **science** in the glossary.
4. **maxims:** concisely expressed principles or rules of conduct, or statements of general truths.

5. **nature:** kind; sort.
6. **rebuff:** repel; refuse; drive away.

An examiner or study partner should examine with exactness on (1), alertness on (2), and seeing if the student understands (3). An examiner or study partner should not go beyond these points, asking for what person was mentioned, who did the test, what is the copyright date, what are the first words, etc.

Irrelevant[7] examination questions only slow the student.

It might also be noted that checkouts on course materials must also ask for demonstrations. Use paper clips, rubber bands, etc. The examiner or study partner should ask questions that require an ability to apply. *Give the student a situation and have him tell you how he would handle it.*

Be as tough as you please, but only on (1), (2) and (3) above.

---

7. **irrelevant:** not to the point; off the subject.

Drill

1. Find another student or a friend to do this drill with. Get a copy of something that both of you have studied and are familiar with. (If there are no materials which you have both studied, then choose something for use in the drill and both of you study it.) Ask the person irrelevant questions about this material and demand that he quote verbatim certain sentences and phrases from it. Write down what you did and what occurred.

2. Now give the other person a standard checkout on the above materials, using the data in the above chapter. Write down what you did and what occurred.

CHAPTER EIGHT:

LEARNING
HOW TO LEARN

The Learning Drill

As has been covered earlier in this book, learning is not always the same as study. Some people can do a whole course and get good marks[1] and not learn anything. A person might pass every exam, yet not have learned the data so that it can be applied.

The following drill is used to improve the ability to study and increase the learning rate.

NAME: The Learning Drill.

POSITION: Student and coach sit facing each other across a table.

PURPOSE: To develop judgment by understanding and duplication.[2]

TRAINING STRESS:[3]

1. *The first step is duplication.*

The coach takes a sentence or phrase from *Alice in Wonderland*.[4] The line used is unimportant. The coach reads it to the student. Coach merely tries to

get student to repeat a line of sounds. You don't need to call them words. It is not rote[5] memory. It is duplication. The coach repeats the line each time the student flubs until the student has duplicated it exactly.

---

1. **marks:** letters or figures used in schools, etc., to show quality of work or behavior; grades.

2. **duplication:** the action of something being made, done or caused to happen again; the action of reproducing something exactly.

3. **stress:** special attention; emphasis; importance.

4. ***Alice in Wonderland:*** a story written in 1865 by Lewis Carroll (the full title is *Alice's Adventures in Wonderland*) about a little girl named Alice who falls down a well into a strange country where very illogical things happen. This book is used as a source of nonsignificant phrases for the Learning Drill.

5. **rote:** in a mechanical manner; by routine.

2. *The second step is understanding.*

After the student has correctly duplicated what the coach read, the coach asks, "Give me an example of that." Student gives example or examples until both are satisfied.

Coach then asks, "How do you feel about that?" and if okay, they continue to the next line. If student has any uncertainties with examples, the coach goes back to step 1 and starts the drill from beginning, using the same line.

If the student still has trouble with examples, coach would ask, "Are there any misunderstoods on this line?" and any found are cleared up. A dictionary should be used.

REMEDY: If the student continues to have trouble with examples, the coach should say, "Give me an example of how the datum isn't that way," and student gives examples until both are satisfied; then, "Give me examples of how it *is*," until both are satisfied. Always end off with how it *is*.

Results

The student should feel good about the datum after duplication and understanding, and should start having realizations as he is further drilled.

Eventually, using the two basic steps, the student will learn judgment.

The drill should be coached on a gradient.

It should be ended on a good success. The student should look good.

The end result on each student is the ability to rapidly and accurately learn data.

Drill

1. Find another student or a friend to do the Learning Drill with you. Have the person doing the drill with you read this section of the book, if he or she hasn't read it before. Do the Learning Drill as laid out in the text first as the coach, then as the student. Write down what you did and what you gained from doing this drill.

Data and Power of Choice

There is another method of education which is quite fabulous. It can help a student to regain power of choice over data.

Here's an example.

Part One

Check before going on if the student can remember the first set of numbers you gave him.

This would be continued until the student could easily recall and repeat a nonsignificant datum.

Part Two

This step is done using examples of nonsignificant data which are totally incorrect. When the student has regained his power of choice, go on to the third step, that of teaching the actual datum you want to teach him.

---

6. **disbelieve:** refuse to believe; reject as untrue.

Part Three

WELL, YEAH, BUT THE DATUM WAS "THE COACH SHOULD **ALWAYS** AGREE WITH THE STUDENT." IS THAT TRUE?
NO, THAT'S NOT TRUE.
ALL RIGHT. NOW I WANT YOU TO GIVE ME AN EXAMPLE OF THAT DATUM USING THESE TWO ITEMS.

This particular method of instruction takes a nonsignificant datum and teaches somebody that the repetition of the datum does not bring about chaos, does not hurt him any, that he can do it.

Then you teach him he could remember it.

You would do this with a nonsignificant datum: one, two, three; a hundred, thirty-two, sixteen. Just numbers. You get a repetition of this, and then he can remember it.

Now, you do something else with him. He's so used to being taught by life with duress, and not with power of choice, that you take a totally incorrect datum. There would be no argument about the incorrectness of the datum. And you let him throw it out. You give him another datum, incorrect, and let him throw it out. If he has any difficulty with the nonsignificant items, you would keep repeating these until he could do it smoothly.

Now you've shown him that he can remember something or reject it, and that is the definition of power of choice.

Then you give him a datum which is the datum you wish to teach him. And you give him power of choice over that datum. But the pitch[7] is to give it a little bit exaggerated in force. "The coach should *always* agree with the student." It's not true.

Let him quarrel with it. Let him chew[8] it around. Let him add it up and look over his own experience.

Make him give you an objective[9] example. That is a vital part of this particular operation—a vital part of it.

Have him set up a dummy situation. If you're teaching him that it is wrong to run off the road with a car, you have him show you where the road is on the table and move the saltshaker off the road.

You give him an objective example. He has to then translate[10] your statement into action. He must do this, and he must continue to do this until he can do it, so that it ceases to be a bunch of words.

---

7. **pitch:** act or manner of expressing in a particular style or at a particular level.

8. **chew:** discuss at length.

9. **objective:** having existence independent of the mind; real; actual.

10. **translate:** change into another form.

Drill

1. Find another student or a friend to do this drill with you. Have the person doing the drill with you read this section of the book, if he or she hasn't read it before. Do the Data and Power of Choice Drill as laid out in the text, first as the coach, then as the student. Write down what you did and what you gained from doing this drill.

False Data

When a person is not functioning well on his job or in life, at the bottom of his difficulties will often be found *unknown* basic definitions and laws or *false* definitions, false data and false laws, resulting in the inability to think with the words and rules of that activity and an inability to perform the simplest required functions. The person will remain unfamiliar with the fundamentals of his activity, at times appearing idiotic, because of these not-defined and falsely defined words.

A politician is told by an adviser, "It doesn't matter how much money the government spends. It is good for the society." The politician uses this "rule" and, the next thing you know, inflation[11] is driving everybody to starvation and the government to bankruptcy.[12] The politician, knowing he was told this on the very best authority, does not spot it as false data, but continues to use it right up to the point where the angry mobs stand him in front of a firing squad[13] and shoot him down. And the pity of it is that the politician never once suspected that there was anything false about the data, even though he couldn't work with it.

There is no field in all the society where false data is not rampant.[14] "Experts," "advisers," "friends," "families," seldom go and look at the basic texts on subjects, even when these are known to exist, but indulge[15] in all manner of interpretations and even outright lies to seem wise or expert. The cost, in terms of lost production and damaged equipment, is enormous. You will see it in all sectors[16] of society. People cannot think with the fundamentals of their work. They goof. They ruin things. They have to redo what they have already done.

False data on a subject can come from any number of sources. In the process of day-to-day living, people encounter and often accept without inspection[17] all sorts of ideas which may seem to make sense but don't. Advertising, newspapers, TV and other media are packed with such material. Even mothers have a hand in it, such as "children should be seen and not heard."

---

11. **inflation:** an increase in the amount of money and credit in relation to the supply of goods and services, resulting in an increase in the general price level. An *inflation* exists where there is more money in circulation than there are goods.

12. **bankruptcy:** the state or an instance of being legally declared unable to pay one's debts (bankrupt): the property of one who is bankrupt is divided among his creditors (those to whom money is owed).

13. **firing squad:** a group of soldiers assigned to shoot someone sentenced to death by a military court.

14. **rampant:** passing beyond restraint or usual limits; unchecked.

15. **indulge:** practice a forbidden or questionable act without restraint.

16. **sectors:** distinct parts of a society or of an economy, group, etc.

17. **inspection:** careful examination.

Where a subject, such as art, contains innumerable[18] authorities and voluminous[19] opinions you may find that any and all textbooks under that heading reek[20] with false data. The validity[21] of texts is an important factor in study. Therefore it is important that any Supervisor or teacher seeking to strip off false data must utilize basic *workable* texts. These are most often found to have been written by the original discoverer of the subject and when in doubt, avoid texts which are interpretations of somebody else's work. In short, choose only textual material which is closest to the basic facts of the subject and avoid those which embroider[22] upon them.

If one is to use at all effectively what one is learning, he must first sort out the true facts regarding it from the conflicting bits and pieces of information or opinion he has acquired. This eliminates the false data and lets him get on with it.

---

18. **innumerable:** too many to count; very many; countless.

19. **voluminous:** of great volume, size or extent.

20. **reek:** are filled with something unpleasant or offensive.

21. **validity:** the state, quality or fact of being valid (well-grounded on principles or evidence) in law or in argument, proof, etc.

22. **embroider:** improve (an account or report) by adding details, often of a fictitious or imaginary kind; exaggerate.

Drill

1. Write down an example you have heard or experienced of false data concerning how to study. Explain how you determined that this was false.

2. Write down how you could help someone else who was trying to sort out the true facts of a subject from the false data about it.

Senior[23] Data

As a person goes through life, he receives data (facts, information) in many ways—from friends, family, school, television, etc.

Not all data is as important as all other data. Some data is more useful than other data and some data is of no value at all.

When one looks at a "sea" of facts, every drop in the sea might look like every other drop. However, since some of the drops of water might be of vast importance, one would need to look for the key data—those drops of water in the middle of the ocean that are the key drops of water.

---

23. **senior:** superior to others in standing (status, rank or reputation).

People have sometimes listened to so many useless opinions in life that they never learn the key data. They then don't have the key data they need to resolve their problems.

Life has certain laws and these are the most senior data of all. The data you get from this book is very basic data which provides you with tools with which you can handle life.

Having these tools in your hands can help you become more causative over life. If you learn to think with these tools and apply them, you will have the senior data which can resolve problems you're faced with. Life will all of a sudden become more livable.

Drill

1. Write down an example you have seen of someone who did not have the senior data in a certain area of his life. How did that person handle this area?

2. Write down three examples of senior data which you have learned on this course.

CHAPTER NINE:

SUMMARY

Summary

The difference between the "bright" student and the "dull" one, the student who is very, very fast and the one who is very, very slow, is really only the difference between the *careful* student and the *careless* student.

The careful student applies the technology of study. He studies with an intention to learn something. He handles any of the barriers to study which appear as he is working with his materials. If he is reading down a paragraph and suddenly realizes that he doesn't have a clue[1] what he is reading about, he goes back and finds out where he got tangled up. Just before that there is a word he didn't understand. If he is a careful student, he doesn't continue until he finds out what that word is and what it means.

That is a careful student, and his brightness on the subject is dependent upon the degree he applies this technology. It isn't dependent on any native talent or anything else. It is his command of the subject of study that makes the difference.

---

1. **doesn't have a clue:** has no idea; doesn't know; is ignorant or incompetent.

About the Author

L. Ron Hubbard was no stranger to education. Although his main profession was that of a professional writer, in a long, event-filled and productive life he spent thousands of hours researching in the education field, lecturing and teaching.

He was born in Tilden, Nebraska on 13 March 1911, and his early years were spent on his grandfather's ranch in the wilds of Montana. As the son of a US Navy commander, he was well on the way to becoming a seasoned traveler by the age of eight, and by the time he was nineteen he had logged over a quarter of a million miles.

He enrolled in George Washington University in 1930, taking classes in mathematics and engineering. But his was not a quiet academic life. He took up flying in the pioneer days of aviation, learning to pilot first glider planes and then powered aircraft. He worked as a free-lance reporter and photographer. He directed expeditions to the Caribbean and Puerto Rico, and later, to Alaska. The world was his classroom and he studied voraciously, gathering experience which provided the background for his later writings, research and discoveries.

Some of his first published articles were nonfiction, based upon his aviation experience. Soon he began to draw from his travels to produce a wide variety of fiction stories and novels: adventure, mystery, westerns, fantasy and science fiction.

The proceeds from his fiction writing funded his main line of research and exploration—how to improve the human condition. His nonfiction works cover such diverse subjects as drug rehabilitation, marriage and family, success at work, statistical analysis, public relations, art, marketing and much, much more. But he did more than write books—he also delivered over 6,000 lectures and conducted courses to impart his own discoveries to others.

However, in order to learn, one must be able to read and understand. Therefore, L. Ron Hubbard tackled the problem of teaching others how to study. His research uncovered the basic reason for the failure of a student to grasp any subject. He discovered the barriers to full comprehension of what one is studying, and developed methods by which anyone can improve his ability to learn and to *apply* the data that he is being taught. He wrote a considerable body of work on this subject, which he termed *study technology.*

L. Ron Hubbard's advanced technology of study is now used by an estimated two million students and thousands of teachers in universities and school systems internationally. His educational materials have been translated into twelve languages to meet this worldwide demand for the first truly *workable* technology of how to study. Organizations delivering L. Ron Hubbard's study technology have been established in the United States, Australia, South Africa, Canada, Austria, Great Britain, Pakistan, Mexico, Germany, Denmark, France, Italy, Venezuela and China.

L. Ron Hubbard departed his body on 24 January 1986. His contributions to the world of education have meant new hope, better understanding and increased ability for millions of students and educators the world over.

Glossary

Alice in Wonderland: a story written in 1865 by Lewis Carroll (the full title is *Alice's Adventures in Wonderland*) about a little girl named Alice who falls down a well into a strange country where very illogical things happen. This book is used as a source of nonsignificant phrases for the Learning Drill.

apostrophe: a mark (') used to show that a letter or letters have been left out of a word (Example: can't [cannot]), or that something is owned (Example: Joe's bicycle).

applications: ways of applying or methods of applying or using; specific uses.

Applied Scholastics International: the organization which promotes and utilizes L. Ron Hubbard's study technology with the aim of restoring educational quality and effectiveness around the world. It licenses and coordinates over 150 educational centers and schools on five continents. For more information, contact Applied Scholastics International at the address in the back of this book.

aptitude: quickness to learn or understand.

arbitrary: derived only from opinion or preference; not based on the nature of things.

archaic: ancient and no longer in general use.

architecture: the science, art or profession of designing and constructing buildings, bridges, etc. *See also* **science** in this glossary.

arrogant: proud and overbearing (forcing others to one's own will) through an exaggerated feeling of one's superiority.

assigns: thinks of as caused by or coming from (a motive, reason, etc.).

axioms: established principles or laws of a science, art, etc. *See also* **science** in this glossary.

bankruptcy: the state or an instance of being legally declared unable to pay one's debts (bankrupt): the property of one who is bankrupt is divided among his creditors (those to whom money is owed).

barriers: things that hold apart, separate or hinder.

biology: the science of living things; study of plant and animal life. *See also* **science** in this glossary.

Bismarck: Otto von Bismarck (1815–1898), German political leader and first chancellor (chief of government) from 1871–1890. Bismarck was called the "iron chancellor"; he fought wars with Denmark, Austria and France as part of his plans to unify Germany.

blow: an instance of a person giving up studying a subject and leaving a course or class.

bogging: being stuck and unable to make progress.

boosted: pushed upward.

brackets: marks ([ ]) used in dictionaries:
(a) to enclose additional information or directions, etc. Example: She said "I wuv [love] you."
(b) sometimes to enclose examples given in the dictionary. Example: *house* 1. a building in which people live [*They are in their house.*]
(c) to enclose the derivation of a word. Example: *pen* [from Old French *penne,* from Latin *penna,* feather]. *See also* **derivation** in this glossary.

buckled down: set to work with real effort.

chase: go in pursuit; follow along.

checkout: the action of verifying a student's knowledge of what he has studied.

chew: discuss at length.

clay demonstration: a training activity done by students as a means of clarifying materials, adding mass to the significance of the materials and working things out. The student is given a word or situation to demonstrate. He does this in clay, labeling each part. The clay SHOWS the thing. *See also* **demonstration, mass** and **significance** in this glossary.

clue, doesn't have a: has no idea; doesn't know; is ignorant or incompetent.

component: serving as one of the elements or ingredients of a whole.

comprehensive: including much.

concept: a thought devoid of (completely without) symbols, pictures, words or sounds. It is the direct idea of something rather than its sound or symbol. *See also* **symbol** in this glossary.

concise: brief and to the point; short and clear.

consult: seek information or advice from; refer to.

context: the words just before and after a certain word, sentence, etc., that help make clear what it means.

correspondence course: a course of instruction by mail, given by a school *(correspondence school)* which sends lessons and examinations to a student periodically, and corrects and grades the returned answers.

counterpart: a person or thing closely resembling another, especially in function.

crude: not carefully made or done; rough.

crushing: overwhelming.

cylinder: a solid or hollow object with straight sides and circular ends.

definition: a statement of the meaning of a word.

demo: short for *demonstration. See* **demonstration** in this glossary.

demo kit: short for *demonstration kit:* a collection of various small objects such as corks, caps, paper clips, pen tops, rubber bands, etc., used by a student to demonstrate an idea or principle. *See also* **demonstration** in this glossary.

demonstration: a practical (having to do with action or practice rather than thought or theory) showing of how something works or is used. Demonstration is used in studying to give the student mass to go along with the ideas studied. *See also* **mass** and **significance** in this glossary.

denotes: is a mark or sign of; indicates.

derivation: explanation of where a word came from originally.

derived: came from a source or origin; originated.

dictionary: a word book. A dictionary contains the meanings of words and other information about them. A dictionary can be used to find out what a word means, how to say a word, how to spell a word, how to use a word and many other things about words.

dimensions: any measurable extents, as length, width, depth, etc. Something which is in two dimensions would have the dimensions of height and width only; in other words, it would be flat.

dinky: *(informal)* small, insignificant.

disbelieve: refuse to believe; reject as untrue.

doingness: the action of creating an effect. By *doing* is meant action, function, accomplishment, the attainment of goals, the fulfilling of purpose or any change of position in space.

doodling: scribbling or drawing aimlessly, especially when one's attention is elsewhere.

dope off: get tired, sleepy, foggy (as though *doped,* or drugged).

dull: mentally slow; lacking brightness of mind; somewhat stupid.

duplication: the action of something being made, done or caused to happen again; the action of reproducing something exactly.

economics: the science concerned with the production and consumption or use of goods and services. *See also* **science** in this glossary.

effect: the receipt-point of a flow (thought, energy or action). For example: If one considers a river flowing to the sea, the place where it began would be the source-point or cause, and the place where it went into the sea would be the effect-point, and the sea would be the effect of the river. A man firing a gun is cause; a man receiving a bullet is effect.

e.g.: for example; from the Latin words *exempli gratia.*

embroider: improve (an account or report) by adding details, often of a fictitious or imaginary kind; exaggerate.

encounter: find oneself faced with.

encyclopedias: a book or set of books giving information on all or many branches of knowledge, or on one field of study, generally in articles alphabetically arranged.

engineering: the planning, designing, construction or management of machinery, roads, bridges, buildings, waterways, etc.

errs: makes a mistake; is incorrect.

etymology: an account of the origin and development of a word and its meaning.

exasperated: angry; very irritated or annoyed.

exclusively: so as to exclude all except some particular object, subject, etc.; solely.

exhibit: show; display.

factor: any of the circumstances, conditions, etc., that bring about a result.

fascists: people who believe in or practice *fascism,* the principles or methods of a government or a political party favoring rule by a dictator, with strong control of industry and labor by the central government, great restrictions upon the freedom of individuals, and extreme nationalism and militarism.

firing squad: a group of soldiers assigned to shoot someone sentenced to death by a military court.

fluently: so as to be able to write or speak easily, smoothly and expressively.

flunk: failure on a course or examination or checkout. *See also* **checkout** in this glossary.

flying: moving or going swiftly.

foggy: not clear; dim; blurred.

frowning: looking with displeasure or disapproval (*on* or *upon*).

geography: of or having to do with the scientific study of the Earth's surface and its physical features, climate, products and population.

glib: characterized by fluency (a smooth, easy flow) or readiness, but implying lack of thought or of sincerity.

gradient: each of the steps in a gradual approach to something taken step by step, level by level, each step or level being, of itself, easily attainable—so that finally, quite complicated and difficult activities can be achieved with relative ease.

grammar: the way words are organized into speech and writings so as to convey exact thoughts, ideas and meanings amongst people. It is essentially a system of agreements as to the relationship of words to bring about meaningful communication.

grasp: get hold of mentally; understand.

groggy: shaky or dizzy, as from a blow, lack of sleep, etc.

guide words: the words written in darker letters at the top of each page of a dictionary which show the first and last words entered on that page. *See also* **dictionary** in this glossary.

hand, to: within reach; near; close.

herein: in this writing.

hesitate: pause; stop momentarily.

hysteria: any outbreak of wild, uncontrolled excitement or feeling, such as fits of laughing and crying.

idiom: a phrase or expression whose meaning cannot be understood from the ordinary meanings of the words.

indulge: practice a forbidden or questionable act without restraint.

inflation: an increase in the amount of money and credit in relation to the supply of goods and services, resulting in an increase in the general price level. An *inflation* exists where there is more money in circulation than there are goods.

innumerable: too many to count; very many; countless.

inspection: careful examination.

irrelevant: not to the point; off the subject.

italics: letters that slant to the right. *These are italics.*

Johannesburg: city in South Africa.

jump: an abrupt change of level either upward or downward.

justifies: shows to be just or right; gives a good reason for; defends.

key: a thing that explains or solves something else, as a book of answers or a set of symbols for pronouncing words.

Leipzig: a city in Germany; the location of Leipzig University, where Wilhelm Wundt and others developed "modern" psychology. *See also* **psychology** and **Wundt** in this glossary.

literate: knowledgeable; educated.

long-winded: speaking or writing at great, often tiresome length.

malady: a disease; illness; sickness: often used figuratively.

marks: letters or figures used in schools, etc., to show quality of work or behavior; grades.

mass: something composed of matter and energy existing in the material universe. *See also* **significance** in this glossary.

math: *(informal)* short for *mathematics*: the science of number, quantity and space. *See also* **science** in this glossary.

maxims: concisely expressed principles or rules of conduct, or statements of general truths.

nature: kind; sort.

nautical: of sailors or seamanship.

navigator: a person who directs the course of (a ship or aircraft or vehicle, etc.).

nonoptimum: not the most favorable or desirable; not the best.

not-comprehended: not grasped mentally; not understood.

objective: having existence independent of the mind; real; actual.

obsolete: no longer used.

obstacle: something that stands in the way or stops progress.

omission: anything which one failed to include; anything left out.

optimum: most favorable or desirable; best.

panorama: range; amount or extent of variation.

paraphrased: expressed (something spoken or written) by putting it into different words having the same meaning.

parentheses: marks [( )] used to put additional information into a statement, a question or a definition. Example: She has the flowers (roses).

parts of speech: the different things words do (name a person, place or thing, show action or state of being, modify or describe another word, etc.).

phenomena: facts or occurrences or changes perceived by any of the senses or by the mind.

pitch: act or manner of expressing in a particular style or at a particular level.

plural: a form of a word which indicates more than one person, place or thing is being talked about.

prime: chief; most important.

principal: first in rank, authority, importance, etc.; chief; main.

pronunciation: the way something is said.

psychology: the study of the human brain and stimulus-response mechanisms. It stated that "Man, to be happy, must adjust to his environment." In other words, man, to be happy, must be a total effect. *See also* **stimulus-response** and **effect** in this glossary.

rampant: passing beyond restraint or usual limits; unchecked.

rebuff: repel; refuse; drive away.

reek: are filled with something unpleasant or offensive.

reelingness: state, quality or instance of having a whirling feeling in one's head; being or becoming confused.

restoration: a bringing back to a former condition.

robotness: state, quality or instance of being a robot, a person who acts or works in an automatic or mechanical way.

rote: in a mechanical manner; by routine.

science: knowledge based on observed facts and tested truths arranged in an orderly system.

sectors: distinct parts of a society or of an economy, group, etc.

semiliterates: people who are barely able to read and write.

senior: superior to others in standing (status, rank or reputation).

significance: any thought, decision, concept, idea, purpose or meaning connected with something as opposed to its mass. *See also* **mass** in this glossary.

singular: a form of a word which indicates one person, place or thing is being talked about.

slang: words or phrases that are not considered to be "standard" in the language. Slang is highly informal language that is usually avoided in formal speech and writing: it consists of both new words and existing words with new meanings and is usually fresh, colorful or humorous, and popular for only a short time.

spinny: dizzy, as if one were spinning.

stimulus-response: of or having to do with a certain stimulus (something that rouses a person or thing to activity or energy or that produces a reaction in an organ or tissue of the body) automatically giving a certain response.

stock: get or keep a supply of, as for sale or for future use.

stress: special attention; emphasis; importance.

stumbles: speaks, acts, etc., in a clumsy or hesitating way.

suits: satisfies; meets the demands or needs of.

Supervisor: the person in charge of a course and its students. The job of the Supervisor is to ensure that his students duplicate, understand and apply the materials of the course being studied. *See also* **duplication** in this glossary.

sweepingly: including a great deal; very broadly.

syllable: a word or a small part of a word which can be pronounced with a single, uninterrupted sounding of the voice.

symbol: something that could represent or stand for a thought or a thing.

synonyms: words in the same language that have a similar meaning to another word in that language. Example: *Big* and *large* are *synonyms.*

tag end: the last or final part of something.

tearing: moving very quickly.

technology: the methods of application of an art or science as opposed to mere knowledge of the science or art itself. *See also* **science** in this glossary.

theory: that branch of an art or science dealing with knowledge of its principles and methods rather than with its practice. *See also* **science** in this glossary.

traced: followed or discovered by observing marks, tracks, pieces of evidence, etc.

translate: change into another form.

undertook: took upon oneself, as a task, performance, etc.; attempted.

unique: limited in occurrence to a given class, situation or area.

validity: the state, quality or fact of being valid (well-grounded on principles or evidence) in law or in argument, proof, etc.

vast: very great in size, extent, amount, degree, etc.

virtually: for the most part; almost wholly; just about.

voluminous: of great volume, size or extent.

Webster, Noah: (1758–1843) American educator and author, best known for his *American Dictionary of the English Language* (1828) and a spelling book called the *Blue-Backed Speller*. A number of widely used dictionaries, of varying scope and quality, still bear Webster's name. *See also* **dictionary** in this glossary.

wind up: *(informal)* arrive in a place or situation as a result of a given course of action.

Word Clearing: procedures used to locate and clear up words the student has misunderstood in his studies.

workable: able to be worked or used or acted upon successfully.

worksheet: a record kept by the Word Clearer during a Word Clearing session of the words looked up and cleared and any other important information concerning the Word Clearing. One uses blank paper, numbering each page consecutively. *See also* **Word Clearing** in this glossary.

Wundt, Wilhelm: (1832–1920) German psychologist and physiologist (expert in the study of the functions of living things and the ways in which their parts and organs work); the originator of the false doctrine that man is no more than an animal. *See also* **psychology** in this glossary.

yet: for all that; nevertheless; but.

Index

For more information on educational books and materials by L. Ron Hubbard, contact your nearest distributor:

Association for Better Living
  and Education International
6331 Hollywood Blvd., Suite 700
Los Angeles, California 90028

Association for Better Living
  and Education Canada
696 Yonge Street
Toronto, Ontario
Canada M4Y 2A7

Association for Better Living
  and Education Eastern
  United States
349 W. 48th Street
New York, NY 10036

Association for Better Living
  and Education Western
  United States
1307 N. New Hampshire
Los Angeles, California 90027

Association for Better Living
  and Education Europe
Sankt Nikolajvej 4–6
Frederiksberg C
1953 Copenhagen, Denmark

Instituto de Tecnologia para la
  Educacion A.C.
Tetla #6 Colonia Ruiz Cortines
Delegación Coyoacán
C.P. 64630, Mexico D.F.

Association for Better Living
  and Education United Kingdom
Saint Hill Manor
East Grinstead, West Sussex
England RH19 4JY

Association for Better Living
  and Education Russia
48 Vavilova Street
Building 4, Suite 169
Moscow 117333, Russia

Association for Better Living
  and Education Australia and
  New Zealand
201 Castlereagh Street
Sydney, New South Wales 2000
Australia

Association for Better Living
  and Education Africa
Security Building, 4th Floor
95 Commissioner Street
Johannesburg 2001
South Africa

Association for Better Living
  and Education Italy
Via Nerino, 8
20213 Milan
Italy

You can also contact any of the groups and organizations on the following pages which use L. Ron Hubbard's study technology.

Applied Scholastics Groups and Organizations

Applied Scholastics International
7060 Hollywood Blvd., Suite 200
Los Angeles, California 90028

United States of America

Arizona
Phoenix Renaissance Academy, Inc.
4330 N. 62nd St., #128
Phoenix, Arizona 85251

Scott Tutoring
4203 N. 9th Avenue
Phoenix, Arizona 85013

California
Ability Academy
PO Box 601091
San Diego, California 92160

Ability Plus School—La Canada
4490 Cornishon Ave.
La Canada, California 91011

Ability Plus School—Orange
County
333 S. Prospect
Orange, California 92669

Ability Plus School—Woodland
Hills
Dept. 503, PO Box 4172
Woodland Hills, California 91365

Academy for Smart Kids
4632 Russell Ave.
Los Angeles, California 90027

Applied Scholastics Compton
11174 Atlantic
Lynwood, California 90262

Applied Scholastics—Crescenta
Valley
7944 Day Street
Sunland, California 91040

Applied Scholastics—Los Angeles
503 Central Ave.
Glendale, California 91203

Applied Scholastics Orange County
701 W. 17th Street
Santa Ana, California 92706

Applied Scholastics—San Francisco
39355 California St. #107
Fremont, California 94538

California Ranch School
17305 Santa Rosa Mine Road
Gavilan Hills, California 92370

Carroll-Rees Academy
4474 De Longpre
Los Angeles, California 90027

Delphi Academy—Los Angeles
4490 Cornishon Ave.
La Canada, California 91011

Delphi Academy—Sacramento
5325 Engle Rd. #600
Carmichael, California 95608

Delphi Academy—San Francisco
445 E. Charleston Rd. #7
Palo Alto, California 94306

Expansion Consultants, Inc.
550 N. Brand Street 700
Glendale, California 91203

Golden Gate Apple School
379 Colusa Ave.
Kensington, California 94707

Karen Aranas Tutoring Center
933 Edward Ave. #24
Santa Rosa, California 95401

Kids Academy
1839 N. Kenmore Avenue
Los Angeles, California 90027

Kids' World School
1220 N. Berendo Ave.
Los Angeles, California 90029

The Learning Bridge
593 4th Ave.
San Francisco, California 94118

Legacy Learning Group
2789 Cornelius Drive
San Pablo, California 94806

Lewis Carroll Academy of the Arts
5425 Cahuenga Blvd.
N. Hollywood, California 91601

Los Gatos Academy
220 Belgatos Road
Los Gatos, California 95032

Mojave Desert School
44579 Temescal
Newberry Springs, California 92365

Pinewood Academy
4490 Cornishon Ave.
La Canada, California 91011

Real School
50 El Camino
Corte Madera, California 94925

Smart Apple Tutoring Service
1310 Chuckwagon Dr.
Sacramento, California 95834

VenturePlan
3300 Foothill Blvd.
Box 12570
La Crescenta, California 91224

Colorado
Applied Scholastics—Colorado
3 Paonia
Littleton, Colorado 80127

Connecticut
Ability Plus Connecticut
256 Brainard Hill Road
Higganum, Connecticut 06441

Standard Education
3 David Drive
Simsbury, Connecticut 06070

Florida
Applied Scholastics—Miami
2557 SW 31st Ave.
Miami, Florida 33133

A To Be School, Inc.
531 Franklin Street
Clearwater, Florida 34616

Jefferson Academy, Inc.
1301 N. Highland Ave.
Clearwater, Florida 34615

Studema International
PO Box 10559
Clearwater, Florida 34617

TRUE School, Inc.
1831 Drew Street
Clearwater, Florida 34625

Georgia
Lafayette Academy
2417 Canton Road
Marietta, Georgia 30066

Illinois
The Learning School, Inc.
864 E. Northwest Hwy.
Mount Prospect, Illinois 60056

Massachusetts
Applied Scholastics—New England
1500 Main Street, Suite 4
Weymouth, Massachusetts 02190

Delphi Academy—Boston
564 Blue Hill Ave.
Milton, Massachusetts 02186

Michigan
Cedars Center
1602 W. 3rd Ave.
Flint, Michigan 48504

Recording Institute of Detroit, Inc.
14611 E. Nine Mile Road
East Detroit, Michigan 48021

Minnesota
Beacon Heights Academy
12325 Highway 55
Plymouth, Minnesota 55441

Missouri
Ability School—St. Louis
14298 Olive St. Road
St. Louis, Missouri 63017

New Hampshire
Bear Hill School, Inc.
PO Box 417
Pittsfield, New Hampshire 03263

New Jersey
Ability School—New Jersey
192 W. Demarest Ave.
Englewood, New Jersey 07631

New York
Maryann's School
#2 Hillcrest
Niagara Falls, New York 14303

Ohio
Applied Scholastics—Ohio
101 W. Dunedin Rd.
Columbus, Ohio 43214

Oregon
Columbia Academy, Inc.
1808 SE Belmont
Portland, Oregon 97214

The Delphian School—Oregon
20950 SW Rock Creek Road
Sheridan, Oregon 97378

Eagle Oak School
PO Box 12
Bridal Veil, Oregon 97010

Pennsylvania
Applied Scholastics Pennsylvania
PO Box 662
Reading, Pennsylvania 19603

Texas
Austin Academy of Higher
   Learning
12002 N. Lamar
Austin, Texas 78753

Perfect Schooling, Inc.
402 Town and Country Village
Houston, Texas 77024

Utah
Ability School—Utah
913 E. Syrena Circle
Sandy, Utah 89094

Virginia
Chesapeake Ability School
5533 Industrial Dr.
Springfield, Virginia 22151

Wyoming
Great American Ski School
PO Box 427
Jackson, Wyoming 83001

Canada
Académie Phénix
9222 Chateaubriand
Montreal, Québec 42M 1X8
Canada

Applied Scholastics
   (National Office)
840 Pape Ave., Suite 209
Toronto, Ontario M4K 3T6
Canada

Berube Educational Services
114 Bourassa
St. Luc, Québec J0J 2A0
Canada

Education Alive—Halifax
2130 Armcrescent West
Halifax, Nova Scotia B3L 3E3
Canada

Education Alive—Kentville
27 James Street
Kentville, Nova Scotia B4N 2A1
Canada

Education Alive—Toronto
840 Pape Ave., Suite 201
Toronto, Ontario M4K 3T6
Canada

Effective Education School
8610 Ash Street
Vancouver, British Columbia
   V6P 3M2
Canada

Progressive Academy
12245 131st Street
Edmonton, Alberta T5L 1M8
Canada

Toronto Ability School
85 41st Street
Etobicoke, Ontario M8W 3P1
Canada

Wise Owl Tutoring
342 Blackthorn Ave.
Toronto, Ontario M6N 3J3
Canada

United Kingdom
Effective Education Association
   East Grinstead
31A High Street
East Grinstead, W. Sussex
   RH19 3AF
England

Effective Education Association
   London
2C Falkland Rd.
Kentish Town, London
England

Effective Education Association
   Scotland
31 St. Katharine's Brae
Liberton, Edinburgh EH16 6PY
Scotland

Effective Education Association
   Sunderland
9 Catherine Tce.
Newkyo, Stanley, Co. Durham
   DH9 7TP
England

Greenfields School
Priory Road—Forest Row
E. Sussex RH18 53D
England

The London Study Center
313 Finchley Road
London NW3 6EH
England

Austria
Kreativ College
Rienosslgasse 12
1040 Wien, Austria

Belgium
Brussels Ability School
Rue Auguste Lambiotte 23
1030 Bruxelles
Belgium

Study Tech Center
Clos des Palombes
1410 Waterloo
Belgium

Denmark
Amager International School
5th Floor, Graekenlandsvej 51-53
2300 Copenhagen S, Denmark

Applied Scholastics (European
   Office)
F. F. Ulriksgade 13
2100 Copenhagen O, Denmark

Applied Scholastics—Denmark
F. F. Ulriksgade 13
2100 Copenhagen O, Denmark

Foreningen for Effektiv
   Grunduddannelse Aarhus
Hammervaenget 22
8310 Tranbjerg, Denmark

Foreningen for Effektiv
   Grunduddannelse Amager
Graekenlandsvej 53
2300 Copenhagen S, Denmark

Foreningen for Effektiv
   Grunduddannelse Birkerod
Kongevejen 110 B
3460 Birkerod, Denmark

Foreningen for Effektiv
   Grunduddannelse Brondby
   Strand
Hyttebovej 20
2660 Brondby Strand, Denmark

Foreningen for Effektiv
Grunduddannelse Bronshoj
Klintevej 40
2700 Bronshoj, Denmark

Foreningen for Effektiv
Grunduddannelse Dania
Daniavej 60 Assens
9550 Mariager, Denmark

Foreningen for Effektiv
Grunduddannelse Dania
Erhvervscenter
Daniavej 60 Assens
9550 Mariager, Denmark

Foreningen for Effektiv
Grunduddannelse Glostrup
Falkevej 20
2600 Glostrup, Denmark

Foreningen for Effektiv
Grunduddannelse Grinsted
Gronlandsvej 2
7290 Grinsted, Denmark

Foreningen for Effektiv
Grunduddannelse Hvidovre
Hvidovre Alle 17
2650 Hvidovre, Denmark

Foreningen for Effektiv
Grunduddannelse Kalundborg
Dalsvinget 5
4400 Kalundborg, Denmark

Foreningen for Effektiv
Grunduddannelse Koge
Straedet 6
Stroby Egede
4600 Koge, Denmark

Foreningen for Effektiv
Grunduddannelse Naestved
H. C. Lumbyesvej 102
4700 Naestved, Denmark

Foreningen for Effektiv
Grunduddannelse Norrebro
Ravnsborggade 6, 5
2200 Copenhagen N, Denmark

Foreningen for Effektiv
Grunduddannelse Norre Sundby
Jorgenbertelsvej 17 A, 1tv
9400 Norre Sundby, Denmark

Foreningen for Effektiv
Grunduddannelse Olstykke
Sajisnej 21
3650 Olstykke, Denmark

Foreningen for Effektiv
Grunduddannelse Osterbro
F. F. Ulriksgade 13
2100 Copenhagen O, Denmark

Foreningen for Effektiv
Grunduddannelse Risskov
Flintebakken 60
8240 Risskov, Denmark

Foreningen for Effektiv
Grunduddannelse Silkeborg
Chr. D. 8. vej 12.1
8600 Silkeborg, Denmark

Foreningen for Effektiv
Grunduddannelse Slagelse
Sct. Mikkelsgade 23
4200 Slagelse, Denmark

Foreningen for Effektiv
Grunduddannelse Tastrup
Kogevej 11
2630 Tastrup, Denmark

Foreningen for Effektiv
Grunduddannelse Vadum
Ulrik Burihovej 69
9330 Vadum, Denmark

Foreningen for Effektiv
Grunduddannelse Vojens
Vestergade 58
6100 Haderslev, Denmark

Kildeskolen
Roskildevej 158
2500 Valby, Denmark

France

Applied Scholastics France
49 rue Général de Gaulle
22400 Lamballe
France

Aptitudes
11 rue Palluat de Besset
42000 St. Etienne, France

Ecole de l'éveil
11 passage Courtois
75011 Paris, France

Institute d'Aide a l'Etude
12 impasse Bonnave
42000 St. Etienne, France

Irene Chartry Tutoring Service
27 rue Andre Cayron
92600 Asnieres, France

Le Cours pour apprendre
16 rue du Bac
75007 Paris, France

Management Distribution
43 rue Volney
49000 Angers, France

Germany

Applied Scholastics—Germany
Unter Buschweg 118
5000 Köln, Germany

Applied Scholastics Aidlingen
Blumenstrasse 14
7042 Aidlingen
Germany

Applied Scholastics Augsburg
Stettenstrasse 36
8900 Augsburg
Germany

Applied Scholastics Cologne
Unter Buschweg 118
5000 Köln, Germany

Applied Scholastics Düsseldorf
Kruppstrasse 45
4000 Düsseldorf 1
Germany

Applied Scholastics Eisingen
Waldpark 2
7531 Eisingen
Germany

Applied Scholastics Euskirchen
Ringelstrasse 14
5350 Euskirchen-Billig
Germany

Applied Scholastics Hamburg
Swartenhorst 50
2000 Hamburg 71
Germany

Applied Scholastics Hünfelden
Obergasse 1
6257 Hünfelden-Ohren
Germany

Applied Scholastics Velbert
Am Neuhanskothen 51
5620 Velbert 11
Germany

Holland

Lafayette School
Vascode Ganver Straat 19
1057 CH Amsterdam
Holland

Italy

Associazione Studio Moderno
Piazza Cittadella, 13
41100 Modena, Italy

Sweden

Applied Scholastics—Sweden
Terrängvägen 39
126 61 Hägersten, Sweden

Daghemmet U-Care
Grusåsgränd 88
122 49 Enskede, Sweden

Fritidshemmet Robin Hood
Terrängvägen 39
126 61 Hägersten, Sweden

Måsens daghem
Nedre Bergsvägen 4
126 34 Hägersten, Sweden

Solrosen
Örtugsgatan 13
414 79 Göteborg
Sweden

Studema-Skolan
Terrängvägen 39
126 61 Hägersten, Sweden

Switzerland
Verein ZIEL
Postfach 5114
6002 Luzern, Switzerland

Australia
Ability Plus
32 Ryan St.
Northcote Victoria 3070
Australia

Applied Scholastics ANZO
319 Canterbury Road
Ringwood, Victoria 3134
Australia

Applied Scholastics—Canberra
36 Ebden St.
GPO Box 1910
Ainslie, Canberra, ACT 2602
Australia

Applied Scholastics—Sydney
Suite 3, Level 3
647 George St.
Sydney NSW 2000
Australia

Applied Scholastics Training Centre
#404, 3 Smail St.
Broadway NSW 2007
Australia

I Can Enhancements
1/23 Glebe Point Rd.
Glebe NSW 2037
Australia

Jenny Gellie Tutoring Services
21 Railway Parade
Hazelbrook NSW 2779
Australia

Yarralinda School
319 Canterbury Road
Ringwood, Victoria 3134
Australia

Japan
Applied Scholastics Japan
3-13-36E 1001
Kusunoki-cho, Nishi-Ku
Hiroshima
Japan 733

Malaysia
Applied Scholastics Institute
No. 42-2A, Jalan Tun Sambanthan
50470 Kuala Lumpur
Malaysia

Pakistan
Effective Education Association—
    Karachi
348 CP Berar Society, Block 7/8
Dhoraji Colony
Karachi-5, Pakistan

Africa
A+ School
28 Church Street
Halfway House
Pretoria 1685, South Africa

Affluence Management
PO Box 59779
Kengray 2100, South Africa

Education Alive—Cape Town
51 Station Road
Observatory
Cape Town 7925, South Africa

Education Alive—Johannesburg
3rd Floor CDH House
217 Jeppe Street
Johannesburg 2001, South Africa

Education Alive (National Office)
3rd Floor CDH House
217 Jeppe Street
Johannesburg 2001, South Africa

Greenfields Education Complex
PO Box 35
Akroso-Akim
Ghana, Africa

Latin America

Colombia
Instituto de Ayuda Escolar
Cra 28 No. 91-39
Sante Fe de Bogotá
Colombia

Mexico
Educacion Del Mañana
Cordobanes 47
Col. San Jose Insurgentes
03900 México D.F.

Grupo Iniciativa
Calzada de Tlalpan #934
Col. Nativitas
03500 México D.F.

ITE de México (National Office)
Tetla #6 Col. Ruiz Cortines
Coyocan
04630 México D.F.

ITE de Guadalajara
Jazmin 376 S.R.
Guadalajara, Jalisco
México

ITE de Jalapa
Corregidora #24-A
Col. Centro
Jalapa, Veracruz
México